TAKE FIVE

TAKE FIVE

Devotions
to Strengthen
a Man's
Life in Christ

EDITED BY
ROBERT BUSHA

BROADMAN
&HOLMAN
PUBLISHERS

Nashville, Tennessee

Printed in the United States of America

4253-68
0-8054-5368-7

Dewey Decimal Classification: 242.642
Subject Heading: DEVOTIONAL LITERATURE // MEN—RELIGIOUS LIFE
Library of Congress Card Catalog Number: 93-45607

Library of Congress Cataloging-in-Publication Data
Take five! : devotions to strengthen a man's life in Christ / Robert Busha, editor.
    p. cm.
   ISBN 0-8054-5368-7
   1. Men—Prayer-books and devotions—English. 2. Christian life—
1960– I. Busha, Robert, 1943– .
BV4843.T355 1994
242'.642—dc20   93-45607
                                            CIP

Honorable men of God are all around me, as are the memories of many more. This volume of *Take Five* is dedicated to all of them.

Rev. Walter Lee Taylor was a greater influence than either of us ever knew from my birth until his death. His memory and influence continue.

The men of Promise Keepers 1993 in Boulder expanded my vision for the responsibilities men are willing to accept.

The men of Grace Fellowship of Santa Rosa have collectively shown more Christian love and willingness to strengthen one another than I've ever experienced before. I'm sure there are many more groups of Christian men just like them. I'm eager to share their faith in God and His hope for our future.

Acknowledgments

Thanks to the staff at Broadman & Holman Publishers, especially our editor, Janis Whipple, for the opportunity to share; and to my wife, Mary Catherine, my collaborator, editor, and continuing source of support and encouragement.

Contents

Put off your old nature which belongs to your former manner of life
and is corrupt through deceitful lusts,
and be renewed in the spirit of your minds,
and put on the new nature,
created after the likeness of God in true righteousness and holiness.

Ephesians 4:22–24, RSV

Introduction

We're everywhere. We meet on Saturday mornings for an hour of learning, sharing, and praying. We get together every Wednesday at lunchtime for Bible study. We gather for weekend retreats by the dozens and hundreds. We meet in small groups in church basements and in massive aggregations as we did for the Promise Keepers conference with 52,000 of us packed into a football stadium. We're in every state and in cities big and small. We come from all denominations.

We're men—Christian men. And no matter what the agenda of our respective gatherings, what we're looking for is spiritual nourishment. The heart of what we're seeking is to strengthen our individual lives in Christ. We want to grow in God.

We have realized that in order to come closer to Him individually, we can't do it alone. So we're coming together to question, to listen, to learn, to encourage one another in our quest.

We know there is, perhaps, no greater challenge for a man than establishing and maintaining a relationship with our Lord. For most of us, the connection seems elusive, except of course when we're in trouble, in pain, or in need of money. Somehow, the events of our days seem to get in the way. Admittedly, it's easier to think about lots of things other than God when our lives are going well. We're realizing this relationship with Him is not easy. We're having to work deliberately to get it right.

In addition to what we gain from sharing, from the strength we get from one another, we seek Him alone. In quiet times. In prayer. In reading and reflecting on His Word. We also look for inspiration in the lives of other men, in their writings, and it is for this reason *Take Five!* has been compiled.

Take Five! offers you the chance to stop for a few moments to hear God through manly experiences, from the trials and tribulations, the pains and the joys of guys who are also struggling to come closer to Him. It's sharing one-on-one in a special way, because every time you read one of these devotions it will take on new meaning. Your needs will have changed from one reading to another, or perhaps your circumstances will have shifted and the words of these contributors will touch you in ways not possible before.

However you consume *Take Five!*—a devotion per day, straight through, as part of a group study—the uplifting potential is immense. May God continue to bless us all.

Robert W. Busha

Dear Lord,
I need to come closer and stay closer to You than I may know how.
Teach me, strengthen me, and show me how to minister to other
men in need as well.
Amen.

If possible, so far as it depends on you,
be at peace with all men.

Romans 12:18, NASB

We Were Right

John Atherton

"Everything will change when she arrives," her husband told me. I had been warned that getting along with her could be rather difficult, but I couldn't believe the words I was hearing. Could anybody be that controlling, that demanding?

Meeting someone for the first time, especially when that person has a relatively bad reputation, can be a real challenge. How would I respond? What would I say?

Her husband was right; she took over the moment she arrived. The dinner menu was immediately changed. We would be eating in the formal dining room, not in the kitchen, she informed us. And we would be using the good china.

It didn't matter that my wife had just cleaned the house. The house needed to be cleaned, she said. For the next hour or so, I thought a white tornado had hit our home.

After dinner we all sat down in the living room to visit. She, of course, initiated the conversation. Talk about family led to a rather sensitive subject, about which she freely gave her opinion. Because the subject dealt directly with my own family, I responded with my thoughts, which just so happened to be in direct disagreement with hers.

Within families there are often unwritten rules. And I had just broken one of those rules: You don't disagree with her. And if you do, you certainly don't say so.

Before I had finished sharing my thoughts, she was in my face, literally, telling me that she was going to have her way. After some heated discussion, she announced that she would be leaving and asked her husband to get their things. And unless we changed our minds—and our attitudes—they would not be returning.

In the months that followed, I spent a great deal of time thinking about that evening and about what had transpired. I knew that we had made a good decision regarding our family's needs. She shouldn't be allowed to control us. We were right, and she was wrong. Yet something plagued me. What was it?

As I prayed, I realized that God was speaking to me about my attitude. Being right and having the right attitude are two different things. After talking with my wife, I decided to write a letter of apology, not because I had been wrong, but because I had had a wrong attitude.

Lord,

help me today to examine my heart's attitude.
Use Your Word and the counsel of godly people in my life to bring correction where it is needed.

Amen.

His divine power has given us everything we need for life
and godliness through our knowledge of him
who called us by his own glory
and goodness.

2 Peter 1:3, NIV

Toaster Power

Harold J. Behm

Our group of engineers was operating a new electric power generating station during an emergency. The plant was sixty miles from our engineering headquarters so we moved into the plant office for the duration of the emergency, eating and sleeping there. We just moved in and made ourselves at home—well, almost at home.

Providing meals for crews on rotating eight-hour shifts was quite a task for the cooks. There was an extra problem with breakfast when we first started. When the cook pushed the handle down on the toaster, the circuit breaker tripped off. The electric circuit to the kitchen simply wasn't heavy enough to power a four-slice toaster. We were amazed. How could there not be enough to power it without blowing the circuit?

This toaster required less than two thousand watts. It was in a building right beside a power plant with two large electric generating units running at full power. These two generating units were producing about 280 million watts. That's enough electric power for a mid-sized city. It's enough to run at least 140,000 four-slice toasters. But we couldn't run our toaster. Why?

We knew the power there obviously was more than adequate. We could hear the continuous hum of the steam turbines driving the large electric generators. The problem clearly wasn't a lack of power. We could draw some power—enough for lighting and for small kitchen appliances. But obviously the connecting wires were not adequate when the demand was heavy. We just didn't have the right connection!

Of course, after we installed a special circuit to supply power to our toaster it performed its assigned task perfectly.

We sometimes have a similar problem in our relationship with the Lord. We read about Him. We know about Him. We may live right beside a church and attend every Sunday. But if we don't have a real commitment to Him, a relationship with Him—the right connection—then we can't receive power from Him to meet the problems we face.

Lord,
help me through the study of Your Word, through worship,
and through praise to build a relationship
based on a genuine commitment to You.
I need this connection through which I can call upon Your power,
not only power to meet my daily needs,
but power sufficient for those times
when the world around me seems in chaos.
Amen.

Make me to know your ways, O Lord;
teach me your paths.

Psalm 25:4, NRSV

A Still, Small Voice

Charles W. Blaker

As a newly commissioned World War II flight instructor, I was returning to home base one evening from a special mission. When the air corridor altered a few degrees to the south, I homed in on the next radio beacon. Navigation lights on. Instrument panel alive in phosphorescent glow. Suddenly everything was blotted out by a suffocating blanket of white. Snow!

The starboard engine coughed. Carburetor ice! Fumbling as though I'd never been in a cockpit, I flipped the heat switch on, pulled the mixture control to full lean, held my breath through an age of seconds until the engine backfired, coughed, snarled . . . and caught!

"Oh, Lord . . . " I whispered. Only then did I hear the rising whine of the engines. A quick glance at the instruments threw me into shock. The altimeter was unwinding, the rate of descent passing through five hundred feet per minute; the artificial horizon was tipped beyond anything I had ever seen; the bank-and-turn indicator registered an uncontrolled spiral skid!

I wondered, "What is the last moment like before the Plexiglas™ canopy rushes toward your face and the ruptured metal skin of the plane slashes at your twisting body?" The snow closed in as I sat, catatonic.

Over the keening engines I suddenly heard laughter. In my head there was a voice, "So why did they teach you to fly on instruments? Don't just sit there, *do something!*" I did.

Thirty seconds later I was straight and level, a thousand feet below where I had been. Although I was off course, still blinded as the snow smothered me, I was now in control.

Before blundering into the storm, I'd passed an auxiliary airfield, with a rotating beacon and boundary markers. Could I get back to it? The voice came again: "Altitude slipping. Nose up a little. Watch the artificial horizon. Not too steep. Add power; she's slipping off the low wing."

And abruptly, I was out from under the storm. Just ahead were the beacon and corner lights of the auxiliary field. I shoved the throttles to full power and raced before the trailing wall of snow; no time to hunt for the landing light switch. Ease down into the blackness. I never felt the wheels touch down, and I somehow knew it wasn't luck!

One Sunday after the war ended, it all came together for me. "The call to service," the minister said, "is not always earth shattering. Rather, it may be a still, small voice, audible only when the chatter of competing voices is stilled. It may be divine intervention disguised as luck, when we confront crises."

It was then I recalled: "So why did they teach you to fly on instruments? . . . Not too steep. Add power; she's slipping off the low wing."

Lord,

help me to filter out the background noise
and hear Your voice.

Amen.

Though I walk through the darkest valley,
I fear no evil; for you are with me;
your rod and staff—they comfort me.

Psalm 23:4, NRSV

Sunrise to Sonrise

Gary A. Bowker

After thirty years of military service, and within days of retirement, the prospect of being helpless was the last thing I expected. But I found myself lying in Bethesda Naval Hospital with pain blotting out any thought of a bright future. The hours of night swallowed my hope, and a relentless throb attempted to rob my soul. Doctors rubbed their chins and muttered over large X-rays, myelograms, and CAT scans. Hypodermic needles found their way into my flesh with the hint that relief would come soon. But relief didn't come. Despair came in its place.

A figure in the familiar uniform of a naval officer appeared beside my bed. She spoke my name like someone who knew me. As I tried to focus, the darkness betrayed my vision. She revealed her identity as a chaplain I'd met. My spirits rose slightly. As she prayed, the words of the Twenty-third Psalm poured over my pain.

"Though I walk through the darkest valley, you are with me; your rod and staff—they comfort me." After the prayer concluded, she stood with me awhile, then quietly left with a promise to return later.

The pain didn't go away, but a candle had been lit deep within me. I knew that if I could only see the rising sun, I could make it another day, and with another day there was hope. Another thought followed, blazing with recognition: In my darkness was the Author of light. The living God was there. The Son has risen to claim me in the hours when I am in the dark valley. In that certain knowledge I endured darkness.

In time, the sun rose and shined its healing light into my room, but it was a brighter Son who had gotten me through. In the days that followed, my health improved.

It's been five years since that night. But the memory still shines on.

Loving God,
in the hours of darkness,
the light of Your Holy Son stands the vigil.
I am never alone.
Grant me the eyes of faith to see in the hours
when my mortal eyes are clouded.
Hold me in Your arms,
and grant me victory in Jesus Christ, my Lord.
Amen.

Make ready a people
prepared for the Lord.

Luke 1:17, KJV

Preparation

Robert Busha

Several times in the past year I've heard commentaries regarding the experiences many families have when getting ready for church. One pastor said if there was hell on earth it was Sunday morning for Christians with kids. With smiles and heads nodding affirmatively the congregation understood. The time between get-up and let's-get-going can be chaotic, with nerves jangled, tempers flared, and everybody's attitude set in a direction exactly opposite from where they ought to be heading.

Another commentator suggested families might avoid Sunday morning problems by actually preparing Saturday evening: by making sure clothes are pressed and ready, shoes are polished, pantyhose are purchased, gas is in the car, even having the table set for breakfast before going to bed. The object of these suggestions is being deliberate about coming to the Lord for church services and all other phases of our relationship with Him.

As a man, this takes on special dimensions for me, with at least two being prominent.

First, when we come to the Lord we need to do more than plop down in prayer, or turn a switch on in our minds to the heavenly channel and expect perfect reception. God's there to hear us, to respond to us in ways that are greater than we can imagine, and perhaps greater than we think we need, but we have to be properly prepared. We have to have an attitude that is conducive to communication, receiving as well as transmitting. And our preparation needs to be thoughtful and deliberate. Actually, it's no different from how we might want our children to be when they come to us. "Calm down," we might say. "Let's talk about one thing at a time," we direct. "Don't just rush in and demand something. Just ask," we tell them gently. "There's no need to carry on. Now, let's discuss it and see what your options are," we guide them. God would probably prefer that we take the same approach when we come to Him.

Second, as the leaders of our families, it's our responsibility to guide each member, to teach and shepherd them in coming to the Lord, especially as we prepare for worship services. We can expect the way we lead them, the example we set, will certainly be duplicated—for better or worse.

Now, it's easy to share these thoughts because they come with serious reflection about the way I didn't always lead my child. It also comes after many discussions with other men recently about our approach to God. We all admit we have much to learn, but we're still willing to share with our brothers in Christ as we're growing.

Dear Lord,
keep me ever mindful of my role as a leader in preparing my family
to be godly men and women. And please guide me in my develop-
ment so that I might come to You in a thoughtful attitude, carefully
preparing my mind and body for a right relationship with You.
Amen.

Feeding in the Wind

John B. Calsin, Jr.

My wife and I recently put up a bird feeder. We both like wild birds, and since it's winter, we know normal sources of food for them are scarce.

We were so excited after putting the feeder up. All day long that first day we watched and waited for birds to flock to the food. We'd used the kinds of seeds that birds usually enjoy and need to strengthen their bodies. But at the end of the day we were disappointed. Only three came.

Several days passed before the food was discovered. Finally one day about nine o'clock in the morning masses of birds found the feeder. Red-crowned house finches, dark-eyed juncos and black-capped chickadees landed on the roof, on the edges of the feeder, on the pole holding the feeder up, and even on the sundeck railings nearby. Carol smiled as she watched them devour the food.

Later in the day, the wind picked up. Since the feeder is in an exposed location, the wind buffeted and tossed it around on the end of its string. But the birds were not going to be kept from eating. In spite of the howling winter wind, they hung on to get the nourishment they needed.

We humans are sometimes like these birds. God puts the bread of life out for us in the form of His Word, to give us the nourishment we need, especially for the wintry days of our lives. But what do we do? Often, we pass it and Him by. We don't take time to feed on His Word by reading it and meditating on it. We flit and flutter around instead of taking time to seek Him.

Let's be more like the little birds and Jeremiah. When we find the nourishment we need, let's hang on, eat, and enjoy it.

Heavenly Father,
I thank You for Your Word.
Help me to read it daily
and to grow in my knowledge of You.
Amen.

Yet those who wait for the Lord will gain new strength;
they will mount up with wings like eagles,
they will run and not get tired,
they will walk and not become weary.

Isaiah 40:31, NASB

Wait a Minute

Tom Carter

Recently my wife and I purchased a touch-tone telephone. We were long overdue for one, but I figured, why replace the old phone if it's not broken? We put our new telephone downstairs in our kitchen, where we make most of our calls. In our bedroom upstairs we still use the old rotary dial phone.

The touch-tone phone has spoiled me and helped bring out my impatience. When upstairs and dialing the old phone, I've actually become so disgusted waiting for the rotary dial to return that I have slammed down the receiver, walked downstairs, and used the new phone. No doubt the time to do that exceeds the time it would take me to dial the old phone, but I've learned to disrespect it as something dinosauric.

To say the least, I have a hard time waiting. When driving, my mind races ahead to figure out which route to my destination has the least number of stops. As a passenger in my wife's car, I've told her, "If you'd gone straight instead of turning, you'd have stopped at only three signs; now you're in for four."

She always looks at me as if to say, "Do you think I care?"

Even waiting for the Lord is nerve-racking for me, while waiting for Him to answer my prayers, to guide, to impart His wisdom, to cause spiritual and numerical growth in the church I serve. But if my experience in the ministry has taught me anything, it's that launching out to serve the Lord without first waiting on Him in prayer is to court disaster.

Jesus waited thirty years to begin His ministry. Maybe He's waited decades for you to trust Him. He's waited all my life for me to learn patience. He's still waiting. I'm still learning.

Father,
by faith, I confess that my waiting time is renewal time.
I need to renew my spiritual strength,
my perspective on life, and my fellowship with You.
Thanks for waiting for me
even when I've been unwilling to wait for You.
Amen.

For you were called to freedom, brethren;
only do not turn your freedom into an opportunity for the flesh,
but through love serve one another.

Galatians 5:13, NASB

True Liberty

Tim Coyle

In our household we have two dogs. One is a golden retriever, the other is a mixed breed. It was our mixed breed, Chessie, that taught me something very important about the true nature of liberty.

From the time we first got Chessie she loved to explore. For some reason, though, the rest of the neighborhood seemed to be more interesting than our yard, which is half an acre and more than enough for her running and playing. Normally Chessie would be on a chain when she's outside. But if she got loose, she was gone. As you might expect, that created problems. Some of our neighbors didn't appreciate Chessie in their yards, and not far from us is a busy street.

I tried everything I knew to get Chessie to stay in our yard. Although she did very well in obedience school, the training didn't carry over very well on this matter. Nothing worked.

Then one day she understood. She finally got the message that she could roam freely and do whatever she wanted within the boundaries of our yard, and there would be no disciplinary action when she was done.

Chessie still may not realize that we don't want her to go beyond the property lines for her own good. There are dangers out there. But now she can run and do whatever she wants. She's safe. And that's what I learned from this dog about liberty. Liberty is the ideal environment in which the Christian life is to be lived. God is free, and we are free because we are created in His image. Therefore, we all have the right to live our lives as we choose. But all liberty has limits, and those limits are spelled out for us in God's Word.

To go beyond those boundaries is not liberty, but license or anarchy. The boundaries are not there to limit our fun, but to protect us and to ensure our greatest happiness. The best thing we can do for ourselves, then, is get to know the Scriptures well and to walk according to them as fully as we can.

Father,
thank You for the freedom that is mine.
Help me not to abuse it,
but to use it to find Your perfect will for my life.
Amen.

The fear of the Lord
is the beginning of knowledge;
fools despise wisdom and instruction.

Proverbs 1:7, NASB

Reproof and Spiritual Prosperity

Jack Cunningham

Crack! Another fifty yards off the tee. Oh, well. What else is new? On this chilly February morning I was playing one of the worst rounds of golf in my life. I was just slapping the ball, sending it not very far and everywhere but straight. One would have thought I'd just taken up the game. My father and cousin were playing with me, along with two friends. Was I embarrassed? You bet I was!

"Come here, Jack," said my cousin, Douglas, at the eighth hole. "Let me show you something that might help."

When my turn came I stood at my ball, concentrated on a blade of grass behind it as he told me, and brought my club back slowly. Pow! My ball rocketed down the middle of the fairway. Again and again I used this technique, and my game prospered. The final nine holes were the best nine of my life!

There was more than just a golf lesson for me on this particular round. I didn't ascend a prideful throne and arrogantly proclaim, "I can figure it out." No, sir. Had I done so my game never would have come together and frustration would have ruled the day as well as my golf game. Fortunately, I didn't play the fool.

When, like a fool, we despise instruction, we may be wallowing in a spiritual rut. We can become spiritually dwarfed. Our Christian walk will be marking time because we don't fear the Lord.

On the other hand, the wise man listens to instruction. He lives with the attitude that he wants to improve his life, to please God better, to show what true Christianity is like. Willingly he listens to fellow believers, even when their reproof may hurt. Because he knows that a hurt now is better than misery later, he doesn't shut his ear to the counsel of the godly. His spiritual life will come together—and prosper.

Dear Lord,
give me a willing heart
and a listening ear
that I might heed godly instruction,
and thereby grow.
Amen.

Who is this
that darkens my counsel with words without knowledge?
Brace yourself like a man; I will question you, and you shall answer
me. Where were you when I laid the earth's foundation? Tell me, if
you understand. Who marked off its dimensions? Surely you know!

Job 38:2–7, NIV

Spiritual Frustrations

James Dobson

There have been a few times in my life when I've made the same mistake as Job, demanding answers from God. One such occasion is a source of embarrassment to me today. It is too personal to relate in detail, except to say there was something I wanted the Lord to do for me that I thought I needed very badly. It seemed in keeping with His Word, and I set out to assure that my prayer was answered. I prayed every day for weeks, begging God to grant this request that seemed to be so significant. I was literally on my face before Him during this time of petition. Nevertheless, He clearly said no! He didn't explain or apologize. He simply shut the door. At first I was hurt, and then I became angry. I knew better, but I was tempted to say with sarcasm, "Would it have been too troublesome for You to have taken a moment from Your busy day to hear the cry of Your servant?" I did not utter these words, but I couldn't help what I felt. And I felt abandoned.

Well, two years went by and my circumstances changed radically. The matter that I had prayed about began to look very different.

Ultimately I realized that it would have been most unfortunate if the Lord had granted my request in that instance. He loved me enough to turn me down, even when I was demanding my own way.

Admittedly, most of our spiritual frustrations do not end with an enlightened, "Oh, now I see what You were doing, Lord!" We just have to file them under the heading, "Things I Don't Understand," and leave them there. In those instances, we should be thankful that He does what is best for us whether or not it contradicts our wishes. Even a reasonably good parent sometimes says no to a child's demands.

If we truly understood the majesty of our Lord and the depth of His love for us, we would certainly accept those times when He defies human logic and sensibilities. Expect confusing experiences to occur along the way. Welcome them as friends—as opportunities for your faith to grow.

Lord,

You know I don't always understand all that You do for me.

I don't always understand Your divine silence.

Please give me the strength of faith

and more mature understanding that You, and only You,

know for certain what is best for me.

And give me the patience to wait for it to happen.

Amen.

But as for me,
I keep watch for the Lord,
I wait for God my Savior;
my God will hear me.

Micah 7:7, NIV

A Faithful Watch

Daniel W. Driver

In August, 1936, an east-bound Great Northern Railroad Company passenger train came into the Fort Benton, Montana, railroad yard. A casket containing a sheepherder was loaded into the baggage car. It was being sent back east for burial.

Shep, a dog of collie strain, watched and whined. He knew his sheepherder-friend-master was in the casket. What he didn't understand was that his companion was dead.

After the casket was loaded, Shep watched the engine blow its steam and move the train out of the railway yard, then Shep turned and trotted away not understanding his master would not return. He didn't realize their friendship had ended.

Every time a train came into the rail yard, Shep met it, eagerly wagging his tail and seeming to say, "Is he here, now?" When the train left, Shep's tail drooped. His master had not returned.

As his vigil became known, many people offered Shep a home, not understanding the old dog's purpose in waiting for his master's return.

Shep joined his master January 12, 1942, when a train ran over him as he was trying to meet it. The wire services carried the story of his death and told of his faithfulness in waiting for his master's return. The employees of the Great Northern Railroad Company erected a monument in honor of Shep.

I'm reminded that, as Christians, we're like Shep. We're waiting for our Master, waiting for the return of Jesus Christ. However, unlike Shep, we have an advantage. If we have Him in our lives, we don't have to wait for His physical return to begin that friendship. It can begin now and with it we'll experience joy and peace. We can know that He will hear us. That knowledge gives us hope.

Dear Jesus,
while I wait for Your return,
help me to be as faithful to You as Shep was
in waiting for the return of his master.
Help me in building my relationship and friendship
with You right now,
and to never give up hope for Your return.
Amen.

But the Lord answered and said to her, "Martha, Martha,
you are worried and bothered about so many things;
but only a few things are necessary, really only one,
for Mary has chosen the good part,
which shall not be taken away from her."

Luke 10:41–42, NASB

The Disposition We Share

Ronnie W. Floyd

Years ago I pastored a church located in a small fishing community on the Gulf coast of Texas. One of my most pleasant memories of living in that area is of the frequent drives I took along the beautiful seashore.

I am not an avid fisherman. However, while I lived in this fishing community there were many times when I went fishing with friends because I was so drawn to the water.

On one occasion I remember going fishing with a friend named Buddy. As we returned to the dock, Buddy yelled for me to tie the boat's rope to a post on the dock. The water was calm, and I tied the rope to the best of my ability. I then scurried around, helping Buddy gather the gear we would take off the boat. As I turned around and started to step over the side of the boat, I realized we were at least twenty feet from the dock. I was one step away from trying to walk on the water. My leg froze in midair, and I was suddenly aware that I had not tied the rope securely. Buddy laughed. Once again he started the boat's motor and guided us to the dock. This time he decided that he would fasten the rope.

I learned a lot by going fishing during those years, but the greatest lesson I learned was how quickly a boat could drift without my realizing it. Even when the water was calm, the boat would drift in a very subtle manner.

At times we also drift from God without even knowing it. Every person can fall prey to the times in which we live. If we are not careful, we will become victims of our circumstances. Our disposition toward drifting is the common denominator we all share. And this tendency can cause us to abandon the goal of living a life connected with God.

Father,
keep me from drifting away from You.
Keep me from being distracted.
Set for me a bold reminder that I am really nothing without You.
Amen.

Now flee from youthful lusts,
and pursue righteousness, faith, love and peace,
with those who call on the Lord from a pure heart.

2 Timothy 2:22–23, NASB

Staying Home

Scott Froese

After my new dog was weaned, I brought him home and began trying to teach him to behave, to be useful, and to do what he ought to do. As he grew he began to broaden his boundaries, until eventually out of concern for his safety I had to chain him up to keep him home. After awhile, however, I realized that chaining him meant that he was only good for eating, sleeping, and being unhappy, so I let him loose. He immediately went back to his old ways, running happily down the driveway and out of the yard to play with his friends and chase cars.

Soon he began staying away for days at a time, coming home only when he was hungry, or when he wanted someone to pet him, or when he needed someone to care for a hurt.

One of those injuries was the result of being hit by a car. He came home whining and dragging his back leg. For a few days I thought he'd learned his lesson. I really looked forward to him being on the front porch when I pulled my pickup truck into the driveway, his tail wagging a big welcome. Before long, however, his leg mended. And as soon as he was well, he was up to his old ways, looking for action, friends to play with, and cars to chase.

He still doesn't seem to realize that if he stays home he'll be fed and petted regularly. He could see lots of action and have a lot of fun walking through the fields and working together with me.

Someday when he's too old to play anymore or is permanently crippled by one of the cars he chases, he'll come home to stay…or perhaps I'll have to scoop him up off the road and bury him.

I can't make him accept the life I intended for him. I can only hope that one day he'll see it for himself, before it's too late.

I think I've seen a little bit of what God goes through!

Dear Father,
help me to keep from straying from Your presence.
My desire is to walk with You in all things…
to enjoy Your fellowship, Your companionship,
and be counted as a friend to You.
Amen.

For whom the Lord loves He reproves,
even as a father,
the son in whom he delights.

Proverbs 3:12, NASB

Take a Lap!

Bruce M. Garner

"Garner, that was pathetic! Take a lap and get in front of the line."

Our coach was a tough and wiry man. He had an intimidating posture and no-nonsense bearing. His immediate response to my performance during a drill sent me scrambling to my feet and running around the field.

When I entered high school, I looked like the "before" photo of an advertisement for muscle building equipment: eighty-nine pounds on a five-foot frame! Most of the girls were taller, heavier, and probably stronger than me. My size was a special challenge because I really wanted to play football.

Along with eighty-five other young guys, I went out for the freshman team. Fortunately, our school had a no-cut policy, so making the team wasn't difficult. However, getting a uniform was a problem. For four weeks I did nothing but run laps and do calisthenics while waiting for enough people to drop out in order for me to get "pads." Finally, the day came and I had a uniform.

To avoid getting severely injured, which the coaches apparently thought very likely, I was rarely allowed to participate in contact drills or scrimmages. I played in games even less. At practice, when I was obviously tired of standing around, one of the coaches would tell me to run some laps. It was an unhappy season, but I stuck it out.

My sophomore year was different. I'd grown some, gotten a uniform right away, and was finally permitted…ah, required…to do contact drills. The coaches were tough, and any mistakes or apparent lack of sincere effort was immediately the cause for laps or wind sprints.

Now, as I ran my lap, sweating and panting, I nearly floated around the field. I felt great. At last, I knew I was part of the team. Instinctively, I knew if I was worth correction, I was worth something.

Correction stings for a short time, but it affirms our worth. God's discipline means we're worthwhile. We're valuable to Him. Without His discipline, and that of His church, we'll never experience a sense of value to God and have our identity in His family.

Father,
I need the affirmation of Your love and my place in Your family.
I submit to Your discipline and ask You to correct me.
Help me to endure its sting,
so that I can also enjoy the reward.
Amen.

Peace I leave with you;
my peace I give you.
I do not give to you as the world gives.
Do not let your hearts be troubled and do not be afraid.

John 14:27, NIV

Calmed by the Lord

Dick Hagerman

Just after breakfast that late October morning, I stood at the back of the bunkhouse, close to the rushing Salmon River. I was donning a down-filled jacket for the chilly jet-boat run downriver to the steelhead fishing holes. Suddenly the cabin shivered. Its floor heaved, and the water pipes rang like a bell in a fire station.

I reached for my woolen cap and said, "The steam's sure shaking the pipes."

"That's not steam," shouted another fisherman named Stan. "It's an earthquake!"

Adrenaline flowed. My heart fluttered like a valve in a high-speed engine. I'd read descriptions about earthquakes but never experienced one.

"So what do we do?" I yelled over the noise.

"Get outside," Stan yelled at me as he opened the door.

I staggered across the rolling floor and down the bunkhouse steps. Across the river huge boulders crashed into the rumbling river. From the

---

31

peaks above the bunkhouse, I expected a boulder to tumble down on us, but none came. It seemed an eon before the earth stopped shaking and a gentle mountain breeze pushed the clouds of dust out of the steep walled canyons. God had calmed His creation.

I stood at the bunkhouse steps until my heart slowed to normal. *The world isn't stable,* I thought. *Nor are its concepts of peace and enjoyment.* Standing on the shaking, threatening earth seemed like living under today's shaking, threatening social and economic pressures. I'd worried about surviving the giant boulders crashing down the mountain canyons just as I worry about surviving business and career decisions.

I remembered how Jesus comforted His disciples, and thought about the peace He left for them. *If God can calm these rumbling mountains and settle the tumbling stones,* I thought, *it's time I let Him calm my rumbling fears and settle my tumbling life.*

Comforting Lord,

let me depend on You to settle my insecure mind.

Amen.

Well done, good and faithful servant!...
Come and share your master's happiness!

Matthew 25:21, NIV

Ministry on Every Occasion

James H. Harrison

Lying in bed, gazing at the ceiling, he said, "Imagine me, here like this!"

Mark had been so full of energy and ministry. He worked with every age group in our church and volunteered his talents to the community. He'd been a friend to so many in need and an angel of mercy to those unable to care for themselves. Now cancer had taken away his energy and vivacious personality.

As church members we came to his bedside to let him know that we loved him and were eager to see him well again. We were taken back when we saw this once spiritually energetic and motivated man diminished so quickly by this cancerous foe. We were at a loss for words. Our journey of mercy, love, and good intentions seemed to turn into awkward uselessness.

As he lay gazing at the ceiling he said once again, "Imagine me, here like this!" But this time he looked straight at us, as if expecting an answer. His eyes moved us. They were the eyes of a man in misery. We didn't even have to think before we answered him with these gentle words:

"You have ministered to many with your talents, love, and helping hands."

"Your compassion and willingness to bear the burdens of others have healed many a broken spirit and heart."

"Your being here like this gives us an opportunity to minister to you."

"See, even now you minister."

The quickness of our answers took Mark back. He looked toward the ceiling once again, but this time it was as if he had transcended the plaster and was looking straight into heaven. He gave a prayer of thanksgiving for his friends and long life in the ministry of his Lord.

The physical pain and weakness were still present, but his useful life was not diminished.

God of all mercy,

thank You for giving me every opportunity to minister.

As Jesus ministered even on the cross,

may I continue to minister on every occasion.

Amen.

Commit everything you do to the Lord.
Trust him to help you do it and he will.
Rest in the Lord;
wait patiently for him to act.

Psalm 37:5,7, TLB

Helping Hands

David P. Hauk

The engine droned monotonously as I continued to push the mower back and forth across the lawn. Although I can't honestly say I hate this chore, I wouldn't put it on my list of favorite things to do. Still, since it is a relatively mindless task, lawnmowing gives me lots of time to think. So, I continued to plod along, row after row, pushing the machine in front of me.

Suddenly, my five-year-old son, Danny, came running into the yard. He rushed over to me and took a spot beside me, placing his little hands next to mine on the handle.

"I want to help you," he yelled over the noise of the engine.

"Okay," I yelled back.

I smiled. *You won't want to come near this thing in another ten years,* I thought.

Within a few minutes I realized Danny's help was only slightly more useful than mine would be to an auto mechanic. Mowing the lawn while holding the mower handle at the level of a five-year-old is not easy.

Although Danny had the impression he was helping, he was actually more of a hindrance.

Suddenly, I felt very sorry for God. I realized He must have this problem constantly. How many of us come to God with a problem or concern, asking Him to take care of it? Then, we try to help Him out by doing things our own way, anyway. We forget that God knows what is best for us.

We needn't try to give God assistance or speed up the process. It's better to give Him our problems and then let Him help us, rather than help Him. We need to wait patiently, knowing that He has the situation well under control.

Lord,
when I come to You with problems and worries
may I remember that Your way and timing are perfect.
Help me to be patient.
Amen.

I press on toward the goal
to win the prize for which God has called me
heavenward in Christ Jesus.

Philippians 3:14, NIV

Discipline

Bill Hybels

Several years ago, I played on a park district football team. During the warm-up before our first game, I learned that I would play middle linebacker on the defensive unit. That was fine with me; my favorite professional athlete is Mike Singletary, all-pro middle linebacker for the Chicago Bears.

The game started. When it was time for the defense to take the field, I stood in my middle-linebacker position, determined to play with the same intensity and effectiveness I'd so often seen in Mike. Scenes of nationally televised Sunday afternoon football games flashed through my mind and psyched me for a major hit.

The opposing offensive unit approached the line to run their first play. Mimicking Mike, I crouched low and stared intently at the quarterback, readying myself to explode into the middle of the action in typical Singletary style. The battle raged...and reality struck with a vengeance. Using a simple head fake, the quarterback sent me in the opposite direction of the play, and the offense gained fifteen yards.

So went the rest of the game. By the fourth quarter I came to a brilliant conclusion: If I wanted to play football like Mike Singletary, I would have to do more than try to mimic his on-the-field actions. I would have to get behind the scenes and practice as he practiced. I would have to lift weights and run laps as he did. I would have to memorize plays and study films as he did. If I wanted his success on the field, I would have to pursue his disciplines off the field.

Discipline is no less important on the field of Christian living. If we want to be like Christ, we have to live as He lived. That doesn't mean we focus on the special moments when His character and compassion shone in the public spotlight or try to mimic Him the way I tried to mimic Mike Singletary on the football field. It means we imitate His entire life, including the behind-the-scenes disciplines that prepared Him to shine when the pressure was on. It means we "practice the activities He practiced."

What are these activities? The disciplines include solitude and silence, prayer, simple and sacrificial living, intense study and meditation upon God's Word and God's way, and service to others.

Dear Jesus,
I want to live like You,
to serve with grace, to resist temptation, to uphold conviction,
to exhibit power in Your name.
Be with me as I seek to discipline my Christ-like endeavor.
Amen.

But He said to them,
"It is I; do not be afraid."

John 6:20, NASB

Pulled Down—Lifted Up

Larry Ladd

The water seemed to swirl around me and the current pulled me below the surface. It's been said that a person's life passes before him when there's sudden danger and the possibility that life may pass away. It's true! I realized just how true one evening at the beach on the Oregon coast.

I'd accompanied my grandparents to visit relatives. As part of our trip we decided to spend a few days at a coastal resort. One morning several of us went starfishing among the rocks on the shore.

The tide was out and the sea creatures clung to the rocks after the waters receded. It was a beautiful site, and gathering the starfish was a great new experience. We decided the beach would be a perfect place for an evening picnic, so plans were made to return later in the day.

While our delicious evening feast was being prepared, I decided to walk alone to the rocks where we had been earlier. I didn't know about the danger that comes with higher tides.

It appeared I'd be able to walk through the water, but now there was no bottom. As I stepped, panic rose within me. With limited swimming skills I began to struggle, but suddenly a quiet voice said, "Be calm. I'll take care of you." Surprisingly, a peaceful comfort settled over me and I was able to regain my senses and actually swim back to dry land. It was only a few feet, but it seemed like a mile. By then my companions had discovered my absence and were hurrying to my rescue.

Some would say this was luck, but I know it was the voice of God that spoke. It was His hand that lifted me from those frightening, dark waters.

As the struggles of daily life try to pull us down and defeat us, we can be saved if we put our life and destiny in the care of Christ, the One who loves us most. I'm thankful for this hope as each new day dawns and each sun sets. Those few minutes on an Oregon coast proved to be a turning point in my life.

Thank You, Lord,
for the peace You give me
in times of trouble and distress.
Be with all those who are facing dark waters
in their daily journeys through life.
Amen.

Take off your sandals,
for the place where you are standing
is holy ground.

Exodus 3:5, NIV

Eternal Instants

Max Lucado

We played every game we knew. We ran up and down the hall. We played "find me" behind the couch. We bounded the beach ball off each other's heads. We wrestled, played tag, and danced. It was a big evening for Mom, Dad, and little Jenna. We were having so much fun that we ignored the bedtime hour and turned off the TV. And if the storm hadn't hit, who knows how late we would have played.

But the storm hit. Rain pattered, than tapped, then slapped against the windows. The winds roared in off the Atlantic and gushed through the nearby mountains with such force that all the power went off. The adjacent valley acted as a funnel, hosing wind and rain on the city.

We all went into the bedroom and laid on the bed. In the darkness we listened to the divine orchestra. Electricity danced in the sky like a conductor's baton summoning the deep kettle drums of thunder.

I sensed it as we were lying on the bed. It blew over me, mixed with the sweet fragrance of fresh rain. My wife was lying silently at my side. Jenna was using my stomach for her pillow. She, too, was quiet. Our second child, only a month from birth, rested within the womb of her mother. They must have sensed it, for no one spoke. It entered our presence as if introduced by God Himself. And no one dared stir for fear it leave prematurely.

What was it? An eternal instant.

An instant in time that had no time. A picture that froze in mid-frame, demanding to be savored. A minute that refused to die after sixty seconds. A moment that was lifted off the timeline and amplified into a forever so all the angels could witness its majesty. It was an eternal instant when the Creator smiled and said, "It is good."

Eternal instants. You've had them. We all have. Such moments are necessary because they remind us that everything is okay. The King is still on the throne and life is still worth living. Eternal instants remind us that love is still the greatest possession and the future is nothing to fear.

The next time an instant in your life begins to be eternal, let it. Put your head back on the pillow and soak it in. Resist the urge to cut it short. Don't interrupt the silence or shatter the solemnity. You are, in a very special way, on holy ground.

Dear Father in heaven,
I have savored the eternal instants You have so generously given me.
I cherish their memory.
Each is an awesome lesson of Your love for me
and a precious reminder that I must love You, too.
Amen.

For we do not have a high priest
who is unable to sympathize with our weaknesses,
but we have one who has been tempted in every way,
just as we are—yet was without sin.

Hebrews 4:15, NIV

The River of Life

Louis Merryman

The water rushed by as we climbed into the five-man rubber boat. Three of us sat in front. Our oarsman sat behind us. A good shove by him got us out into the fast moving current. Our two-hour float trip down Utah's Provo River began at high speed.

This wasn't a thrill-a-minute white water raft trip, but we were glad we had someone at the oars who knew the river. When the river narrowed, we rushed through; when it widened, we slowed down. And there were always unseen dangers.

Actually, there were more hazards than thrills. We had to duck our heads under three bridges. We gave wide berth to the Provo pedestrians we called trout fishermen. And we had to be alert for the assorted logs and sharp rocks that could deflate our craft.

Each turn and twist brought a new view of the river and a panoramic glory of the Wasatch Mountains. As we floated past trout fishermen we asked them if they'd caught any fish. Some had. Some hadn't. One fisherman hooked one as we went by.

Our raft trip seemed to me like the passage of time. The river moves on moment by moment. Once a moment of time is gone it's gone forever and can't be recaptured. Each moment has its beauty and an environment wherein we must function. Then, we move on to another moment and new surroundings. Some dangers are easily recognizable like the rocks or logs that rise up above the river, while others are hidden, except for the pattern of swirling waters which hint at the danger below. There are also moments when we can relax.

Our raft trip taught me two things. First, each moment of time, like each stretch of river, must be lived to its fullest. Second, as a Christian I can rely on the Skilled Oarsman, Jesus Christ. He knows the route I must follow. He's met the dangers, the joys, and the temptations of the river before. He'll get me home safely.

Thank You, Father,
for Your Son, Jesus,
who became man and understands my sorrows,
my joys, my pain, my smiles, and my temptations.
Thank You for the fact
that He can be my oarsman on the river of life.
In Jesus' name.
Amen.

Trust in the Lord with all your heart,
and do not lean on your own understanding.
In all your ways acknowledge Him,
and He will make your paths straight.

Proverbs 3:5–6, NASB

Trust in Him

Dennis V. Meyers

I was flying in clouds at seven thousand feet. I could barely see the wingtips. The plane began bouncing around a little, and then more. At first, I was thinking about how well I was doing. But after a few moments, the icy fingers of fear began to wrap themselves around my heart. The hair on the back of my neck started to rise. A cold sweat broke out on my forehead.

My senses were screaming that I was in a slow, descending bank to the right. A spiral! I desperately wanted to pull up on the yoke and bank to the left, but the memory of my instructor's voice was speaking to me. "Remember, believe your instruments! Your feelings can deceive you!"

Okay. I checked the turn and bank indicator; straight and level. The rate of climb and descent indicator was holding steady on zero. The altimeter was fluctuating around seven thousand feet. All the instruments indicated the aircraft was not in a spiral.

At that moment of recognition, the plane broke from the clouds into the clearing. The sun never looked better. With all the visual references restored, I confirmed what the instrument panel indicated. I was flying straight and level, maintaining altitude.

Many times our Christian walk is like this. We're in the clouds of life. We don't know what's going on. Our feelings tell us, "My life is out of control. I'm not going to make it!" We doubt what God has planned for our lives. But the Lord says, "Trust the instruments of My Word, the voice of My Spirit. Keep your eyes on Me; don't go by your feelings!"

When we follow those instructions, sure enough, we see things are just fine. He *does* know what He's saying to us.

Lord,
help me trust with all my heart
and to keep my eyes totally on You.
Amen.

And my God shall supply all your needs
according to His riches in glory in Christ Jesus.

Philippians 4:19, NASB

But now abide faith, hope, love, these three;
but the greatest of these is love.

1 Corinthians 13:13, NASB

God, My Provider

Timothy M. Peter

It seems the holiday seasons are sometimes the most difficult of times. In December, a few years ago, I went through a terrible period of depression. It was a time when I felt unwanted, unloved, and rejected. I desperately craved attention that I felt I was not receiving, and I was willing to go to any extreme to get it. I even seriously considered suicide. I didn't really want to die, however; I just wanted to be noticed.

I later realized there were many people who loved me, and they went out of their way to show me they cared about me. But at the time, I needed to be told I was loved, not just shown. I believed words and actions must go together, and I was not getting the combination I thought was needed.

As I was studying my Bible one night during that period of depression, I came across two Scripture verses, and I put them together. God promised me in Philippians He would meet all my needs. I, and many others I know, usually take this verse to mean God will provide finances or other material needs. However, in Corinthians, God said love is the greatest thing we could have. Through combining these two verses, I realized God would provide for even my emotional needs.

That night I confessed to my best friend I would no longer limit God's promise only to fulfilling financial or material needs. Several nights later, I spoke with another close friend about my near-attempt at suicide, and he gave me a little project to work on. He had me write down the names of everyone I could think of who I knew cared about me. After several minutes, I filled the front side of a large piece of paper. Now, I keep that paper in the front of my Bible where I can look at it and remember God has given me many people who care about me.

Dear Lord,
thank You for promising to meet all my needs,
both material and emotional.
Please help me daily to remember You love me
and that You will provide others who will love me
with the love You give.
Amen.

Whoever wants to become great among you must be your servant,
and whoever wants to be first must be your slave—
just as the Son of man did not come to be served,
but to serve, and to give his life as a ransom for many.

Matthew 20:26–28, NIV

Becoming New People

Gerry Presley

Several times a week I visit a coffee shop on the way to work. Invariably, there's a man sitting on the curb—long bearded, poverty stricken—waiting for people to give him money or something to eat. Once in a while I'll see him with a cup of coffee, but nothing more. He sleeps on a piece of cardboard in the park. For months I've walked past him. I've never spoken to him.

Originally he was forty or fifty feet away from me, more out on the edge of the parking lot. In recent weeks he's moved over and is right next to the driveway. When I walk past him now, I'm only two or three feet away. Each time I walk by he looks up. I know he wants something, but I just keep walking. The last time I walked by, he looked up and spoke to me. "Do you have money for a cup of coffee?" I shook my head and walked on.

When I did that, something inside of me really hurt. It was as if I'd gotten to know him, but I was still indifferent. I knew at the time, by the poignancy of the moment, that God was dealing with me about this situation and that He would come back to it. Sure enough, that night during my devotional time, He came back to it. However, I didn't really have it clear in my heart until the next morning in worship service, when the whole scene returned to my mind. Very clearly and without any misunderstanding, God spoke to my heart and said, "Don't do that again. Don't just walk past that man anymore."

There are things that God wants to do in our lives. There are ways He wants to speak to us that go beyond our reasoning or beyond our understanding. We just *know* that He's speaking to us, that He wants to deal with us, and that He won't let go until we understand. I want to acknowledge that God is working in my life. I want to be prepared for it, and be ready to receive His messages.

I won't walk past that man on the curb anymore. I don't know what God will direct me to do. But I do know I won't walk by him. That's how God works: He's transforming us into *new* people.

Father,
increase my sensitivity and response
to the needs of those around me—
needs that are obvious and those that may not be apparent—
that I may become a servant of all.
In Jesus' name.
Amen.

Be of the same mind toward one another;
do not be haughty in mind,
but associate with the lowly.
Do not be wise in your own estimations.

Romans 12:16, NASB

A Humble Heart

Jason Presley

I was surprised when Dr. Hart invited me to join him at one of his Russian Orthodox church services. At the university, a hierarchical gap separated the students from the professors, and rarely did they interact outside the academic setting. But Dr. Hart, the only orthodox professor on an evangelical campus, had the reputation of being very *unorthodox* at times—breaking unspoken codes.

I had thoroughly enjoyed Dr. Hart's Russian literature class the previous semester and, having developed an interest in Russian culture, I jumped at his invitation. I knew this was an occasion few students ever experienced. Every student of literature at our school revered Dr. Hart's brilliance.

On the way to the church, I thought about the Russian Orthodox rituals and doctrines Dr. Hart had often mentioned in the literature class. The ceremonial high church approach to worship greatly differed from my own modern nondenominational background, and I soon realized I was a bit nervous about attending an orthodox service.

My nervousness doubled when I arrived. Outside, solemn nuns and priests in black robes hurried about quietly. Inside, the walls were covered with icons of various saints, apostles, and the Godhead. Numerous candles glowed in the melancholy atmosphere and the sickly sweet scent of incense filled my nose.

All during the service, priests recited long prayers in a peculiar sing-song manner, which irritated me to no end. I tried to remain a student of culture, but I quickly found myself judging their foreign ways.

However, just at the point when I had decided to mentally withdraw, I realized I was the only one still standing. The rest of the congregation had simultaneously prostrated themselves on the floor. I had no doubt what this action signified, and a sudden sense of shame overwhelmed me. While they had been praying, praising, and repenting, I had been comparing, judging, and elevating myself. My judgment fell to their convicting repentance, and I knew I was the one who needed most to fall prostrate before God.

That night, I suffered the fate of the Pharisees and swallowed a bitter pill of spiritual pride. And from that point on, I saw Dr. Hart in a different light. I saw a humility underneath his academic prowess that disrupted the professor/student hierarchy. I saw more than a professor, more than a brilliant man; I saw Christ.

Lord,

teach me the humility that shuns greatness
in the eyes of my fellowman.
Slow my quickness to judge,
and speed my understanding that You are a God
who transcends all forms of worship
and inhabits the praises of all Your children.
Amen.

But those who hope in the Lord
will renew their strength.

Isaiah 40:31, NIV

Praying when Life Is Unraveling

Harold Sala

How do you pray when your world is falling apart? Or, like some, do you stop praying, believing that God has ignored you or forgotten that you exist? It's easy to become frustrated and to have thoughts about giving up when our world seems to be coming unraveled, and we are powerless to stop it. It can be a painful and lonely time. But we know there is reason to be faithful and have hope.

Prayer is based on a relationship of the child with the Father. The apostle Paul explains that God has sent forth the Spirit of His Son into our hearts who cries, "Abba, Father!" That plea which rises from the heart of God's child is prayer! It's just that simple.

Prayer isn't demanding things from God or ordering Him to send the golden spoon of wealth as we strike a deal with Him. It isn't telling Him about all the wonderful things we will do for Him and His kingdom just as soon as we are able to bank His blessing.

Prayer is not demanding things from God, but asking of the Father a blessing in simple, childlike faith.

God does hear and answer the faintest plea of His children, but His answers are far deeper than our human understanding. Simply put, God answers in four ways.

First, some answers are direct. Seemingly, the request and the answer move along in parallel channels. That's the way we like prayer. We ask and immediately receive what we've asked for. Frankly, God often gives those kinds of answers to new believers so they understand that He is the Almighty and His power knows no limits.

Second, some answers are delayed. In this case, it's a matter of timing; God answers on His timetable, not ours.

Third, some answers are disguised. We ask for something, and later look back and recognize how God answered. But His answer was different from our request, and we recognize how much better His answer was.

Fourth, some answers are denied. He loves us too much to give us everything we ask for. I've lived long enough to be able to look back and say, "Thank You, Father, that You said no to some of my requests."

Father *does* know best, and you can trust Him for His best in your life.

Thank You, heavenly Father,
for the knowledge that You are just a prayer away.
Amen.

God of Primroses, God of Hope

Brad Sargent

"Yup, spring's on its way," my dad said. "The primroses will be up and blooming soon!"

Oh, no, not the primroses again, I groaned inwardly. His cheery comments about his favorite plants were a source of irritation to me.

Dad's stroke five years earlier left him weak and it impaired his sense of balance. It forced him to retire at age fifty-six. His new daily routine consisted of simple chores like shaving and making his own breakfast and lunch.

My problem, a serious infection, had put me in bed a full month and required an extremely long recuperation period. Now my dad and I sat at the kitchen table, both battling physical ailments. The similarities ended there.

When I looked outside at the winter scene, I saw only a thick carpet of snow, naked cherry tree branches quivering to a cold wind, and gray skies. It seemed, too, my fight against this illness would never end and my hopes for the future would remain forever frozen.

When Dad peered through the picture window, he saw something totally different.

He saw reason for optimism and expressed it clearly! "Snow's melting. Won't be long now 'til we see primroses peeking through."

How he loved those hardy little clusters of leaves and flowers. Although he couldn't plant them on his own anymore, in the spring someone else would dig holes, place baby primroses into them, and scootch the dirt back around the plants. Then it was Dad's turn.

Laboriously using his aluminum walker, he made his way to the mounds, and then he would step on the soil to pack the plantlings. Later he'd stand on the patio and spray them with mist from the garden hose. What joy their array of colors gave him all summer and autumn.

It's been many years since that kitchen scene and several since Dad passed away. I'm well now, and as I look out on the backyard, I finally understand why the primroses were so important to him. They symbolize hope during winter, the assurance of springtime to come.

Hope, like Dad's primroses, takes work to plant and careful cultivation to foster growth. Then hope requires patience and endurance—we must wait and watch for the blooming. At the proper season, full enjoyment will come as our reward.

Lord Jesus,
You are God of the primroses.
Help me remember that beneath my bleak struggles
and confusion lies the truth of Your coming.
Grant me a warmed heart and the strength I need
to endure until spring.
Amen.

If we live by the Spirit,
let us also be guided
by the Spirit.

Galatians 5:25, NRSV

Sing It with Spirit

Scott Sibley

The guest organist obviously didn't know what was going on. But we choir members did. We'd been through it many times before.

After the organist finished playing "Blessed Assurance," our minister stepped forward to conduct us through the chorus one more time. We knew the music and lyrics by heart, so we looked up from our hymnals to watch for direction from our conductor. He guided us through the music, adjusting the timing, bringing out the chords, emphasizing some phrases, keeping us moving through others, drawing out the music from each individual, so we blended together well.

We sang the same hymn both times. The words, notes, chords were all the same. But the second time, with a leader guiding and emphasizing our performance, we produced a much more beautiful, exciting, and inspiring finish for our worship service.

In order to sing with the conductor's guidance, we need to know the music and the lyrics. The conductor is not going to change the notes, but we need to raise our eyes from the book to look at him. We need to understand and follow the direction he gives us. He will show us what to emphasize, and will adjust the timing for us as necessary. He will bring out the beauty of our talents, and we'll blend well with those around us.

The Lord has given His Word and His Spirit to lead us through life. We need to get to know His Word. Then we need to watch for His Spirit's leading and be ready to follow. The Spirit puts life in our work and shows us how to blend with those around us. And the result will be a glorious performance!

Lord,
thank You for giving me Your Spirit to lead me.
Keep me open to Your leading and Your timing
so that I can blend with the work
You are doing through those all around me.
Amen.

Visiting the iniquity of the fathers on the children,
on the third and fourth generations…
but showing lovingkindness to thousands,
those who love Me and keep My commandments.

Exodus 20:5–6, NASB

No More Shame

Lester W. Smith

Many of us come from dysfunctional family backgrounds. My own roots include alcoholism on both sides of the family. Because of the devastation I saw in the lives of my relatives, I made a deliberate effort to avoid any alcoholic beverages or illegal drugs. There was no way I was going to be an addict, too!

One day I went with some relatives to the race track. It was fun and no one in the group got carried away in their betting. It seemed like such an innocent family outing, yet when I woke up the next day, I knew I was hooked!

Every day I returned to the track or paid a coworker to go for me and place my bets. One night, however, I finally came to my senses. I realized I'd become just as addicted as other family members were addicted to alcohol. My addiction was gambling.

I cried out to God for mercy and then placed a crazy bet. Without regard to the identity of the horses in the race, I bet the first three numbers of my phone number and promptly left without watching the outcome.

My prayer was that if I won at such a long shot, I promised to never wager again. It was the reckless request of a wayward, immature, twenty-year-old. If I were God, I don't think I'd have responded to such a foolish petition! Yet, the next day, when I read the race result in the sports section of the newspaper, I discovered I'd won! I collected my winnings at the track and never returned. All the money I lost betting on horses had been recovered. And when a coworker tried to pay me for a bet he had lost, I refused it. He was shocked to hear I was through wagering forever. The Lord made sure I'd placed my last bet.

Lord of all grace and mercy,
thank You for the power of Your Spirit
to break chains of addiction in my family.
Amen.

The effective prayer
of a righteous man can accomplish much.

James 5:16, NASB

Mama Left Me a Legacy of Prayer

Robert C. Smith

My mama, Lena, was known all over the community as a "church going woman" by sinners and a "prayer warrior" by Christians. Both titles fit her perfectly, but if I had to chose between those two descriptions, I would chose prayer warrior. Mama not only went to church; she prayed continually!

Every night, when I was a child, she prayed with me and for me at my bedside. This instilled in me the value and worth of prayer. Even today, my first reaction, especially in a difficult situation, is to pray.

I can still remember one of the first prayers Mama taught me: "Now I lay me down to sleep, I pray the Lord my soul to keep. If I should die before I wake, I pray the Lord my soul to take."

Just as Jesus taught His disciples how to pray by actually praying in their presence, so Mama taught me. The effect that her prayer life had on me time will not erase, nor ages destroy. I still recall the sacred and solemn words of Mama's prayer as she commenced the devotional period at one Wednesday's prayer meeting:

"Lord, I am calling on You this morning not because You are hard of hearing, nor because You are far away, but I am calling You because we need You, Lord! Here we are as empty vessels waiting to be filled. We need You right now, Lord. Lord, have mercy upon us. Your mercy will suit our case this morning."

When Mama finished praying, you could feel the presence of God all over the church.

Mama prayed about everything. When I got sick, she didn't have money to take me to the doctor, so she prayed—her "cure all treatment." No matter what the problem, she would lay hands on me—rubbing me—and pray. Yes, Mama taught me prayer as a way of life.

I believe the influence of Mama's prayers were a buffer against some of the perils of peer pressure when I was growing up. Every time I attempted to do something wrong, in my mind I could hear Mama saying, "Lord, keep him in Your will; don't let him stray; make him what You want him to be, even if You have to break him."

Materially, Mama died a pauper, but spiritually she died rich. She didn't leave me material goods but she left me a legacy of prayer. Thanks, Mama, for leaving me a legacy of prayer.

Lord,
thank You for praying mothers.
Amen.

Although they know God's righteous decree
that those who do such things deserve death,
they not only continue to do these very things
but also approve of those who practice them.

Romans 1:32, NIV

A Downward Spiral

Charles R. Swindoll

Some of my most pleasant memories take me back to a little bay off the Gulf of Mexico. My maternal granddad owned a small cottage on the bay and was generous to share it with his extended brood. Throughout my adolescent years our family spent summer vacations there: boating, swimming, jumping off piers, seining for shrimp, early-morning fishing, late-night floundering, but mainly laughing and relaxing.

However, while those years passed in family togetherness and fun, an ugly erosion was taking place. The waters of the bay were eating away at the bank of land between the cottage and the sea. Year after year, thanks to the rising and falling tide, a few hurricanes, and the lapping of waves at the shoreline, chunks of earth were being consumed by the bay. In all our busy activities and lazy hours of relaxation, no one ever talked about it or bothered to notice. In my childish innocence I never even thought about it. But I shall never forget the day that changed. I did a little experiment late one summer day that made an indelible impression on my mind.

The previous year, our class in junior high school had studied erosion. The teacher did a good job of convincing us that even though we cannot see much happening or hear many warnings, erosion can occur right under our eyes. So, all alone the last day of our vacation that summer, I drove a big stake deep into the soil and then stepped off the distance between the stake and the sea—about fifteen feet, as I recall.

The next year we returned. Before sundown on the first day we arrived, I returned to the stake and stepped off the distance; a little under twelve feet remained. The bay had gobbled up another three-plus feet—not in big gulps, understand, but an inch here and another inch or so there during the year that had passed. I've often wondered if I ever returned to that place of happy family memories, would the cottage still be standing, or would it have surrendered to the insatiable appetite of the sea?

My interest is not simply with a cottage…not nearly so much as with character. Ever so slightly, invisible moral and ethical germs can invade, bringing the beginning stages of a terminal disease. No one can tell by looking, for it happens imperceptibly.

The same downward spiral can impact a family. What is tolerated by Mom and Dad flows down to son and daughter. The tragedy is that it doesn't stop there. Those kids grow up, shaping a nation's future.

Lord,

keep me ever vigilant to the erosion that can occur in my life.
Remind me that there is risk for my family, for my nation,
and for the body of believers.
Amen.

Dear brothers,
is your life full of difficulties and temptations?
Then be happy.

James 1:2, TLB

Mistakes, Accidents, & Other Blessings

Richie G. Thomas

Years ago I visited an art museum in a metropolitan city. Of all the great art, there is one that stands out in my memory. It was, in fact, trash. Bottle tops, broken pieces of glass, doorknobs, machine parts, and such were fastened together within a frame that covered an entire wall. In front of this "work of art" was a small sign informing me that the title of the work was *Victory* and that it was best viewed from a distance.

I moved along and made the circuit in the museum looking at the other paintings and sculpture. Finally, at the far end of the display hall I remembered the "junk" and turned to view it at the recommended distance. Suddenly it appeared that in place of the trash collection someone had hung an incredible picture of an eagle, clutching in its beak a limp, vanquished snake. The colors were so vivid; the image so lifelike. To my amazement I realized the masterpiece and framed junk were one in the same.

The isolated events of our lives often lack obvious value. Our circumstances viewed at close range seem more a hodgepodge than a design. It takes some faith to think that God assigns a value to these throw-away days. The design of life and the value of our isolated circumstances are best understood from a distance. Perhaps a week from now or a month from now or a year from now you'll look back and appreciate the beauty of the design.

Sometimes I think the only place to stand to measure the true beauty of life is at the throne of God.

Father,

teach me to appreciate the symmetry of history's design.

Teach me to see myself and the clumsy, painful,

awkward events of my life as a part of that design.

Grant me the grace to participate

in Your plan with confidence and thanksgiving.

Amen.

Steering Me Through

Russel J. Wagner

I awoke in mid-air just before the impact. I was off the road traveling sixty-miles-an-hour through a ditch. I tried turning the steering wheel to the left, attempting to get back up onto the roadway. Instead, the car spun sideways. Finally I managed to get it straightened out and kept it that way until I came to a halt some two hundred feet later.

I'd been driving across the country for over twenty hours straight. This was the last leg of my journey, only an hour more to go. Although I knew it was foolish and risky to be driving that long without sleep, I trudged on mile after mile, cranking the windows down and cranking the radio up to help keep myself more alert and awake. I thought, *I've got it under control.* I'd come this far, and wouldn't let a minor detail like sleep slow me down. Sitting in that ditch, however, it became crystal clear that my judgment had failed me.

I immediately thanked the Lord for my miraculously safe landing and then looked around to assess the damage. The inside of the car was a shambles, its contents strewn all over. Stepping outside, I noticed the wheel alignment was all out of whack. Yes, this lesson was going to cost me dearly.

Thankfully, the station wagon (obviously not intended for off-road driving) was still driveable. Wide awake from the surge of adrenaline in my system, I continued to drive on and arrived safely at my destination. Praise the Lord!

Reflecting on this eye-opening experience brings to mind similarities in my relationship with God. How many times have I found myself alone in another ditch in my life without a clue as to what happened or how I ended up there? I've been wrecked and badly in need of repair. It happens when I rely on my own judgment to guide me; when I think I have things *under control.* Must my landings always be so rough, my repairs so costly?

God wants the steering wheel to my life. I know He doesn't always steer me clear of all of life's inevitable roadblocks and chuckholes, but He *will* guide me through them and allow me a sense of peace and certainty during the trip.

No, it's not always easy turning over total control of my life. But when I think of where I might end up on my own, I'd rather, with His help, keep to the straight and narrow road, the one that leads to everlasting life.

Lord,
thank You for steering me through difficult times,
and for catching me when I fall.
And thank You for Your Son,
who will never let me fall asleep at the wheel.
I pray I never take my eyes off You,
and will continually be in Your Word,
so as to avoid unnecessary crashes.
Amen.

His work will be shown for what it is,
because the Day will bring it to light.
It will be revealed with fire.

1 Corinthians 3:13, NIV

Treasure or Trash?

Mark Weinrich

We found a perfect arrowhead on a cave floor on our last trip searching for these kinds of finds. So, on our next trip to the same site, we anticipated discovering other Indian artifacts. We were disappointed when we found nothing in the cave.

In our haste to get back home we almost passed another find—an enormous skull lodged in the dirt and debris next to the trail. Only an eye socket protruded above the ground. We dug it out and wondered: What could it be?

"Maybe a Giant Sloth!" I said. We named it "Sammy."

We lugged our cumbersome discovery over a mile to the car. Then we drove to the home of the rancher on whose property we'd found the skull. We invited him to inspect our find.

The rancher looked at Sammy and then at us. He took off his hat and rubbed it with his fingers. We waited expectantly for his judgment.

"Sorry, boys," he said, "but that's just the biggest draft horse skull I've ever seen! I wonder how it got up there?"

Our heads sank and our faces registered our deep embarrassment. The rancher quietly strolled back and closed the door to his house. We figured he probably leaned against the door to support himself because the force of his laughter might have caused him to fall to the floor.

That was a hard day to live down in our small town. Some of my friends still delight in mischievous reminders of our great discovery.

The old draft horse skull traveled as far as a pile of junk behind my house to continue its decay. Sammy had been a treasure for a brief time.

Most of us will see how futile our treasures on earth have been when we stand before the Lord, but some of us have had the humbling experience of finding out on earth.

My partner in the great "Sammy escapade" wrote me during his junior year in Bible college, "I am learning that the only worthwhile things are those that are done for His kingdom and all else is worthless. I want my life work to amount to more than a pile of trash that will be burned on the last day."

Father,
help me to invest my life in people and in things
that will have eternal benefit.
Amen.

He will teach us his ways,
so that we may walk in his paths.

Isaiah 2:3, NIV

Traveling Country Roads

W. Peter West

Our annual vacation is a cherished event for our entire family. As we plan for it with faith, hope, and more than a little love, we know this time away from our usual routines will be filled with pleasant learning experiences.

During our last summer vacation all had gone well. For our own three children and a friend they brought along, as well as ourselves, sailing, swimming, fishing, water-skiing, volley ball, and long nature walks had torn away urban tensions.

Now Sunday had come, and with it a trip to a rural church, which we reached after going through winding country lanes. I tried to mark in my memory the route our friends took leading the way in their station wagon. I invited our children to do the same.

When the worship service was over, we decided to leave before our friends did. "Do you know the way back?" they asked. The children shouted in unison. "Of course, we do!" We set off with the children as our guides.

"Turn right at the barn, Dad!"

"I remember this crossroad. We turned left here," said our guest.

They seemed to recognize every marker, every turn in the road, almost every tree, until we finally came to a dead end . . . literally! It was the entrance to a cemetery!

The children groaned. "We're lost!"

My wife wondered how we would ever get back in time for lunch, since there were no houses nearby and no farmers in the fields to ask for help.

"All is not lost," I said rather smugly. "Our host for lunch, Jim, gave me a map to get back to their cottage. I remember exactly where we started to go wrong. Let's go!"

The children quickly learned the lesson. When going through unknown places, it's good to have a map to supplement your memory; a *reliable* map! They soon cheered up, and following written directions, we arrived home in time for lunch.

O Lord Jesus,
it is wonderful to know You have a plan for my life,
and have provided me with the Scriptures
as a guide to use for all the new and unexplored journeys of life.
Amen.

But when the kindness of God our Savior and His love for mankind appeared, He saved us, not on the basis of deeds which we have done in righteousness, but according to His mercy...
that being justified by His grace we might be made heirs according to the hope of eternal life.

Titus 3:4–5,7, NASB

This One's on Me

Gene Wilder

At age six, I learned one of my first lessons about grace. The day was unusually hot as I walked into the country store. Eagerly, I reached into the cooler and pulled out a cold, wet bottle of Coca-Cola.™ With boyish pride I marched to the cash register and plopped my nickel and penny on the counter. The owner playfully thumped me on the head and smiled as he rang up the purchase.

As I stuck the neck of the bottle into the opener it happened: the bottle slipped from my hands! My boyish treasure struck the floor and was instantly dashed to pieces. Though I tried to hide them, the tears of disappointment trickled down my flushed cheeks.

My friend, the store owner, seemed relatively undisturbed. Without a word, he retrieved a mop and quickly cleaned up the evidence of my carelessness.

The word *disappointment* is not strong enough to describe my feelings as I walked from the store empty-handed. As I began to leave, however, the owner called my name.

"Gene."

When I turned, I saw he was offering me another Coke!™

"I don't have any more money."

My smile climbed almost as high as his friendly eyes as he replied, "Forget it, son. This one's on me."

On that hot summer day I received this valuable lesson about grace. I was given what I thought I didn't deserve. I was given the second treasure even though I had ruined the first. I'm still learning.

My Lord still gives me far more grace than I probably deserve. My life continues to be surrounded with blessings I could never obtain by myself. As an adult, I still break things I treasure. Thankfully, I have a loving Father who cleans up my messes and replaces my broken treasures with new ones from His abundant supply, and, when I ask why, He just smiles and says, "Forget it, son. This one's on Me."

Every now and then, when I think of God's grace I feel like a first-grader who dropped his Coke™ and drank it, too.

Dear Lord,

no gift is more precious than the gift undeserved.

Thank You for second-chance gifts.

Please help me to make the most of all the gracious gifts I receive.

In Jesus' name I pray.

Amen.

Fight the good fight of faith;
take hold of the eternal life.

1 Timothy 6:12, NASB

Crisis Training

David Wilkerson

What kind of fight have you been putting up lately? Have you been overwhelmed? Are you discouraged, perplexed, wounded?

I remember a time when I was standing at a window overlooking New York City. I really saw nothing, but I heard voices. On one side a death angel whispered, "Your daughter has cancer—she's next!" And on the other side Satan whispered, "I'll wreck your home and cause you to reproach His name!" Everything seemed to be unraveling. My body was heavy with pain, fear, and trembling.

I know what it's like to scream at God: "What's going on? I'm not living in sin. I've obeyed You! I came to New York in faithfulness to You. I haven't done anything to deserve this. Is this what happens when I obey You? If I've done wrong, show me." I was suffering—and to make matters worse, the Lord didn't come to me with outstretched arms of comfort. I heard no soft whisper of reassurance. Instead, He came at me with fists clinched, commanding me, "Stand up, David. Fight!" God wanted to be my sparring partner!

Think about this: Suppose a boxing trainer takes his fighter to a training camp, then spends the whole time psyching him up for the big fight. He tells the boxer: "You don't have to suffer through hard workouts. I'll be with you at ringside. I say you're going to be a winner! When you step into the ring with Monster Man, don't worry, my word is all you need."

What kind of trainer would do this? A foolish one! A good trainer would get the best boxer he could find and put him in the training ring with his man.

The Lord needs well-trained fighters—and right now He's doing a quick work in His remnant. It's called crisis training! God is putting Holy Ghost fight in His warriors and He's bringing forth men and women who are tested and tried. The more they suffer and the more intense their trial, the greater the work He has for them to do.

God wants to raise up a people who aren't concerned only about making their own living, owning a house, or driving a nice car. He's seeking those who are greedy for the blessings of God—not to consume on themselves, but to be used of Him to help others!

God is calling you today to get your eyes off your circumstances. You can't judge anything by your present condition. Don't try to figure it out—just accept that you're being trained. Throw off your passive, defeated countenance. Cast aside all feelings of defeat. Stand up and fight!

Lord God,
don't let fear and uncertainty cast me down.
Meet me in prayer. Give me strength.
Help me to be trained and ready for battle.
Help me to stand up and fight.
Amen.

Be still,

and know that I am God.

Psalm 46:10, NIV

Be Still

Grayson F. Wyly

We were a U.S. Army Signal Corps team on a secret mission. I was the commanding officer. Much of our travel was to be over desert terrain in California, so I checked out a three-quarter-ton truck from the motor pool.

While traveling alone through Death Valley, I stopped the truck and walked up one of the small knolls. No wind was blowing. The bushes were motionless, and so was I. The vastness of the valley swallowed up any sound that was made. It was then that I realized the truth of the saying, "It's so quiet you can feel it."

It was quiet, *really* quiet. There was no flash of lightening, no earthquake, no burning bush, not even a still, small voice. But I knew the Lord was there. He'd created it all, from the tallest mountain peak to the smallest grain of sand. At that moment, I knew for certain He knew me inside and out. To be known so perfectly was a sobering thought.

We all need such times of quietness to become more deeply and intimately acquainted with God, the great I AM. So often we're taken up with the busyness of our lives that we fail to see our need in the stillness of eternity.

To have a quiet time each day takes purpose, desire, and discipline. God speaks to us at such times through His Word. We should commune with Him then in prayer.

Yes, communing with Him in prayer sounds simple enough, yet it's amazing how much persistence it takes to do it consistently. That's why we have to work at it deliberately. We have to look for every opportunity. For example, have you ever awakened in the middle of the night for no apparent reason and wondered why?

At such times, it's good to pray and to praise God for who He is and what He's done for you. Also, try asking the Lord what you should do about certain problems you face.

Seek His will, and you'll be amazed at the wisdom of the solution.

May the prayer of the psalmist David be ours as well:

O God,

Thou art my God; I shall seek Thee earnestly;

my soul thirsts for Thee, my flesh yearns for Thee,

in a dry and weary land where there is no water.

Psalm 63:1, NASB

I have learned that everything has limits;
but your commandment is perfect.

Psalm 119:96, TEV

Fences

Harold J. Behm

There seemed to be fences everywhere on the Winding Trail Farm—miles of fences. Every field, orchard, barn lot, and garden was enclosed by a fence. But why so much of it? Fencing is expensive.

I didn't fully realize the significance of these fences when I was growing up on the farm, but my mother did. She knew quite well the value of a fence, especially the one around the farmhouse yard. Fences established boundaries—boundaries that kept the farm animals in their place, and out of grain fields, orchards, and gardens.

The fences were all in place when I first started to explore the farm. As a small boy, I knew just how far I dared go, and usually I obeyed. I didn't have to make a decision whether I should cross the roadway, for example. The wrought iron fence around the farmhouse yard decided that for me.

Even when, on occasion, I strayed beyond those clearly designated limits, I knew without any doubt where the limits were. Mother didn't have to say to Dad, "Hal sneaked across the busy road today. We must build that fence around the yard that we talked about last month." No, the fence was already there. It was there before I was born. I knew when I went beyond the fences, my mother would worry. I didn't fully realize the significance of these fences until many years later.

Dad was nearing retirement and wanted to lighten the work load, so he gradually sold off all the animals on the farm. The fields were rented to a neighbor who grew corn, wheat, and soybeans. There really was no need anymore for fences, so they were all removed. The eighty-acre field was no longer surrounded by one-and-a-half miles of fence.

Even when I was much older, and the fences no longer represented real limits for me, I was surprised how I was still affected. Boundaries that had been there for years were gone, but those fences still represented something quite real in my life.

I wonder how lost I would be as a man if I hadn't had the experience of farm fences as a boy. I feel sorry for boys who grow up without fences. It must be frustrating to grow up with no boundaries, with no limits.

Lord,
I pray that You would guide me now
as my mother did when I was a boy.
Keep me mindful of fences and boundaries that I must not cross.
Make me aware of limits that I must not go beyond
for my well-being and the good of those around me.
Amen.

I will lie down and sleep in peace, for you alone,
O Lord, make me dwell in safety.

Psalm 4:8, NIV

Tall Water and a Troubled Night

Gary A. Bowker

Sometimes life comes with such a torrent of events and requirements that we are thrown a little off balance.

As I write these words they are influenced by the literal flood from which my wife and I just returned. A visit to my mother over the Thanksgiving holiday placed us in the midst of the worst flood in the state of Washington in over one hundred years.

Mother's home is located directly on the Skykomish River in Sultan, Washington. On Friday, the Skykomish River rose to its highest level in twenty-five years, and by Saturday it had risen to the highest level in this century. By Sunday morning it crested at the highest level since records have been kept. Nobody was ready for the catastrophic power of the river.

Sandbags stored for emergencies were quickly exhausted. Roads normally used as detours during lesser floods were covered with water. Food sources were out of reach. Help came only by helicopters and boats. People huddled together wondering what the hours ahead would bring. Radio messages were grim. Reality was almost overpowering.

On a huge old tree in Mother's front yard is a prominent knothole three feet above the river. As the night continued I walked to the river's edge again and again to check the rate of its rise. Somewhere in the dark hours of early Sunday morning the water stopped rising; the old knothole was just barely visible.

By dawn the angry waters had dropped a foot, and by 9:30 A.M. the level had dropped another two feet. Mother's home was spared, but the homes of many others were not.

After the danger passed I heard Mother speaking on the telephone. The caller had inquired of this frail little lady, "Were you afraid?"

"No," she replied with characteristic courage, "I had my son with me. The house might have gone, but I was safe!"

For that same reason the flood of life's demands need not overwhelm us, because in the midst of the flood we celebrate the presence of God's Son. Troubles may rage like flooding rivers, but deep inside the spirit is calm because God dwells with us, full of grace and truth, offering a secure refuge.

Oh, Lord,
amid life's surging struggle, grant peace in my soul.
As rivers rise and troubles threaten,
be my comfort, consort, and guide.
Amen.

God is my strength and power:
and He maketh my way perfect.

2 Samuel 22:33, KJV

Then There Was Me

Robert Busha

The opportunity demanded an intensely creative, diplomatic, and physical effort; about two thousand hours in four months with an absolute deadline. Accepting the challenge also meant being four hundred miles from my home and family with almost no connection except by telephone. However, it promised to be a valuable personal and professional investment. Actually, the work was a mix of irregular exhilaration and increasing drudgery. Sunday mornings were the only sure time of relief. My refuge was in a church that looked like an old stone fortress. It was a formidable haven.

About three months into the campaign, the wearies descended on me, along with a world-class case of self-pity. The next Sunday I went directly to my usual pew. I was too tired to pray or think. I was numb. The next hour was a blur.

After the service I deliberately waited to be the last one to be greeted by the pastor. He always gave inspiration. I thought maybe there'd be a boost for me, too. When I reached the line, and looked toward him, I was stunned. The mental punch reverberated to my heart and deep into my guts. The scene took but a mega-second to be recorded in my mind forever.

The man reaching up and shaking hands with the pastor had no legs! His torso, which rested on a four-wheeled tray, looked like that of any older and blue-suited businessman. His countenance was warm. His smile radiated.

Next stood an equally sharp gentleman with just one leg! Between his crutches was balanced the comparatively short figure of a person who fit the image of a retired professor from the local university. Caring. Attentive. Studious. I sensed him to be in love with life and appreciative of the privilege of being part of it.

Behind him teetered an old man a few inches shorter than me who was severely crippled by rheumatoid arthritis. I knew of him from other members of the congregation. His hands were turned stiffly inward and his back arched forward. He walked rigidly on his heels. But he was at peace with his place in our world.

And, then there was me, last in line, first in self-pity. The meaning was instantaneously clear: I would never feel sorry for myself again. If it should happen, I must remember these men and how grateful they were to be alive—and how minuscule my problems would be by comparison. It was a powerful lesson.

Dear Lord,

thanks for caring about me.

Thanks for so carefully molding my attitude

and guiding my development.

You are my refuge and my strength,

and I appreciate the opportunity to share that message with others.

Amen.

*We are destroying speculations and every lofty thing raised up
against the knowledge of God, and we are taking every thought
captive to the obedience of Christ.*

2 Corinthians 10:5, NASB

Under Arrest

Tom Carter

"You're under arrest!"

I could hardly believe my ears. The police officer was talking to *me*. Through the loudspeaker in his patrol car he ordered me to pull my car over to the side of the road.

"Throw your keys out the window and get out of the car!" he shouted.

Within two minutes there were five police cars surrounding me. Guns were aimed at me from all directions. A crowd was gathering.

A kidnapper in that area of town had just received his ransom and set his female prisoner free. She'd given the police a description of the car. It matched mine! To my relief, when they brought her to identify me, she wagged her head back and forth, saying, "No, that's not him." So they let me go.

At first I thought it was kind of fun to be part of the action. Then I began to worry that some of the onlookers might recognize me as a local pastor and not understand that the whole episode was a mistake.

Soon thereafter I ran across the apostle Paul's words in 2 Corinthians 10:5. The memory of how serious the police were when they'd taken me captive stood in marked contrast to my efforts to bring my thoughts captive to Christ—thoughts of ambition, pride, anger, jealousy, hatred, and lust. It was a pretty sorry comparison.

When I should be shouting, "You're under arrest!" I often allow my thoughts to roam freely in the territory that could be marked "Disobedience to Christ." That's the tough part about Christian living; it applies not just to my acts and words, but even to my thoughts. The authority of my Lord Jesus extends to every part of my life, right down to the heart.

The Pharisees of Jesus' day never learned that lesson. Their religion was a matter of doing all the right things and avoiding all the wrong things. God had their words and works, but not their hearts. And without their hearts He didn't have them. What a loss.

I want to be more than a Pharisee, more than even a believer or a Christian. I want to be a disciple of Jesus Christ, to be completely under His wonderful arrest.

Lord,

only when my mind is captive to Your obedience will I be all Yours.

I surrender my mind to Your authority,

in the name of Him who surrendered Himself to the cross

for my sake.

Amen.

Give, and it will be given to you;
good measure, pressed down, shaken together, running over.

Luke 6:38, NASB

You Can't Outgive the Lord

James Dobson

My dad was the original soft touch to those who were hungry. He was an evangelist who journeyed from place to place to hold revival meetings. Travel was expensive, and we never seemed to have much more money than was absolutely necessary. One of the problems was the way churches paid their ministers in those days. Pastors received a year-round salary but evangelists were paid only when they worked. Therefore, my father's income stopped abruptly during Thanksgiving, Christmas, summer vacation, or any time he rested. But that didn't stop him from giving.

I remember Dad going off to speak in a tiny church and coming home ten days later. My mother greeted him warmly and asked how the revival had gone. Eventually, she would get around to asking him about the offering.

"How much did they pay you?" she asked.

I can still see my father's face as he smiled and looked at the floor. "Aw..." he stammered. My mother stepped back and looked into his eyes. "Myrt," he said, "the pastor there is going through a hard time. His kids are so needy. It just broke my heart. They have holes in their shoes and one of them is going to school on these cold mornings without a coat. I felt I should give the entire fifty dollars to them."

My good mother looked intently at him for a moment and then she smiled. "You know if God told you to do it, it's okay with me."

Then a few days later the inevitable happened. The Dobsons ran completely out of money. There was no reserve to tide us over. That's when my father gathered us in the bedroom for a time of prayer. He prayed first. "Oh, Lord, You promised that if we would be faithful with You and Your people in our good times, then You would not forget us in our time of need. We have tried to be generous with what You have given us, and now we are calling on You for help."

A very impressionable ten-year-old boy named Jimmy was watching and listening very carefully that day. *What would happen?* he wondered. *Did God hear Dad's prayer?*

The next day an unexpected check for twelve hundred dollars came for us in the mail. Honestly! That's the way it happened, not just this once but many times. I saw the Lord match my dad's giving stride for stride. No, God never made us wealthy, but my young faith grew by leaps and bounds. I learned that you cannot outgive God!

Dear God,

thank You for teaching me so many years ago Your lesson in giving. And Your Word is as true today as it was when it was written.

"Give, and it will be given."

Amen.

Be diligent to present yourself approved to God
as a workman who does not need to be ashamed,
handling accurately the word of truth.

2 Timothy 2:15, NASB

Feeling for the Floor

Scott Froese

As a little boy, I was usually swinging my feet from the church pew trying to touch the floor. Each Sunday I would contort my body into the most awkward and uncomfortable positions trying to reach my goal: that faraway floor.

It became almost a ritual, much like keeping track of the height of a child with marks in the doorway. Each week or month I mentally marked my growth.

Through the years, as I sat back in the seat I could feel the progress; first the tips of my toes would touch as I swung my legs under the seat, then the front part of my foot found the solid floor. I can't remember the day that I could sit upright and have my whole shoe touch the floor. It just dawned on me one day that what I had wanted so much, and had tried to accomplish with various acts of contortion, had actually happened as the result of a constant, steady, but nearly imperceptible, growth process. The only part I played in that process was to eat properly, providing my body with the nutrients it needed to grow.

Spiritually, I've grown in the same way. At first it was just enough for "the tips of my toes" to touch. Then I worked on touching "the front part of my foot," toward eventually being able to stand and walk with God.

And, just like my physical body, the only way to increase the pace is to "eat right," providing my spiritual body with the necessary nutrients of God's Word. Someday I look forward to my feet touching firmly, being rooted and solidly grounded in God.

Father,

my heart's desire is to know You and walk with You.

As I study and learn,

ground me that I may walk

with my feet solidly on the path of righteousness.

Amen.

Let us therefore draw near with confidence to the throne of grace,
that we may receive mercy and may find grace
to help in time of need.

Hebrews 4:16, NASB

A Terrifying Expectation of Judgment

Bruce M. Garner

When I was about nine years old, my mother baked a cake for my sister's birthday. Mom made wonderful cakes with fancy little curly things that stick up in the frosting.

I didn't know where Mom was when I came in to get a drink of water, but I saw the cake. I've always liked frosting. I looked at those things on the cake and thought, with great longing , "I could nip one off, and no one would know." I nipped one. It tasted really good. I decided you really couldn't tell the thing was missing. Secure in that thought, I went outside to play.

Sooner than the first time, I got thirsty. After I got my drink, I nipped off a few more things. No one could tell those things were gone.

The next time I came in from playing I wasn't there for water. I got so engrossed in nipping things off the cake, I didn't realize what happened. Now, anyone could tell the things were gone! I hastily tried to repair the cake, but I just made it worse. I even ate more frosting. It was hopeless. I fled!

This time I didn't go out to play. I was cowering, terrified of what my mother was going to do when she got hold of me. I stayed outside until I heard her calling. You see, I knew all along there'd be an accounting of all the kids for the missing frosting. When asked, I told her, "I don't know anything about it." Of course, that made it worse.

Other than not touching the cake in the first place, I now know it would have been best to walk right up to her and say: "Mom, I ate the frosting. Kill me now. But I know you won't kill me, 'cause you love me."

As adults, rather than confessing to God what we've done wrong, rather than running to Him and asking for His mercy, we cower. We even hide from Him in prayer and hide from Him in church. We don't voluntarily stand up for an accounting because we have this terrified expectation of what He'll do when He gets hold of us.

But we know that's not God's way. That's only the way of our childish imagination. God's mercy surpasses His judgment just as my mother's did. God will continue to give us grace and He'll do it mercifully, even if we mess up a really good cake.

Father,

help me not to flee from You, but to run to You,

openly admitting my weaknesses and failures.

Forgive me, cleanse me,

set me free from that terrifying dread of judgment,

and help me know Your love and mercy.

Amen.

Casting all your anxiety upon Him,
for He cares for you.

1 Peter 5:7, NASB

Intensive Care

Larry Ladd

It was 4:05 P.M. My life was about to undergo a powerful experience. Suddenly, there was tremendous pressure in my chest, the beginning of a heart attack. Within the next hour the doctor verified my intuitive conclusion, and I was placed in the intensive care unit of a local hospital.

Intensive care quickly had an added meaning for me. Not only was this a clinical experience, it also became a spiritual event as God's *intensive care* guided the medical staff and covered me with His comfort and love.

All my life I've known that I am in the hollow of God's hand. Now, in the physical protection of the ICU, His warm and tender arms were wrapped around me.

There was strength to submit to treatment and assurance that His will would be done. There was nothing to fear. It was God's way of saying that He needs my attention and my gratitude. My life began to take a new direction, working and witnessing for Him. What an opportunity for the Lord to minister to me and for me to share His intensive care with others!

Yes, we can grow spiritually through a misfortune in our lives if we allow God to work in us, for us, and through us. As we look to Him for strength and comfort we will never be alone in our daily walk. In spite of the intensity of our crisis, regardless of the degree of difficulty in our walk with Him, we will experience joy while in His *intensive care.*

Father,
thank You for Your promise to care for me
in times of anxiety, sorrow, and joy.
I turn to You for spiritual and physical healing
so that I might, in turn, minister to others.
Amen.

Then I saw a great white throne and him who was seated on it.
Earth and sky fled from his presence,
and there was no place for them.
And I saw the dead, great and small, standing before the throne,
and books were opened.

Revelation 20:11–12, NIV

Common Sense

Louis Merryman

My first experience on jury duty in Los Angeles was typical of the way things are in southern California. There is always a big *little extra*. It's kind of like when the price of a hot air balloon ride includes breakfast, or when runners in marathons find tables of fruit, bottled juice, and yogurt at the finish line—something unexpected and often pleasant. As an L.A. County juror, I had my own parking spot and shuttle service.

Actually, I became a panel member before I became a juror. You see, major criminal cases devour seventy-member panels with ease before a jury of twelve is selected. In routine matters, a panel consists of twenty-four people. Television courtroom dramas rarely include jury selection. It's a dull and mundane part of the process unless you're directly involved.

Before I became a sworn juror, I sat on three panels. In two of them I had to tell a room full of strangers who I was, where I lived, and what I did for a living. The judge, the prosecutor (in criminal cases), and the defendant's attorney all had a go at me with additional questions. There were moments when I wondered if I were the one on trial.

In another part of the judicial process I heard three different judges say that in their courtroom they interpreted the law. Right or wrong, what they said in their courtroom was the law.

My job as a juror was to pay attention to the facts of the case, deliberate on them, and answer the questions posed by the judge. We were told that what was required was "common sense." With that instruction from the judges, I got my best *little extra.*

During my jury experience one of the absolute facts of life came to my attention. Someday there is going to be a Great White Throne of Judgment. This won't be a jury trial. God will be the judge and what He says will be the law. The book that is opened will be the Book of Life. If my name isn't listed, I expect to be back in the lake of fire. So "common sense" tells me I had better make sure my name is written in that book.

Heavenly Father and Judge of the universe,
thank You for redeeming me through Your Son
so that I will be found guiltless before Your judgment.
Help me to live a holy life before You.
In Jesus' name.
Amen.

I meditate on Thee in the night watches.
For Thou hast been my help,
and in the shadow of Thy wings I sing for joy.
My soul clings to Thee; Thy right hand upholds me.

Psalm 63:6–8, NASB

Meeting My Needs

Jason Presley

In a matter of hours, my responsibilities as a resident advisor had intensified. The wind-driven fire threatening the Pepperdine University campus in October 1993, spread panic among the students, and it was my job to keep them calm and on campus. I located each student and informed them about the situation while giving directions and counsel.

Despite my instructions, it was apparent that most of the residents had no intention of staying on campus. People began frantically packing their cars and screeching out of the parking lot as fast as they could.

A dismal sense of failure was beginning to set in when I got the call to evacuate the dorm as soon as possible. I looked out of my window and saw flames cresting the ridge. After rounding up the few residents still there and sending them to the gym, as we were directed, I grabbed my most important possessions and followed everyone out.

Once in the gym, my responsibilities were dramatically reduced. I had time to reflect on what had just happened. When I looked at my small pile of belongings and realized I could have grabbed all of my stuff, as nearly everyone else had, and had plenty of time to escape had I not been the RA, I struggled not to become angry and bitter.

The reports of the fire sounded bad. I felt my spirits drop, but for the sake of the residents still there, I had to maintain my composure. The emotional sacrifice superseded all else, yet inside I cried, "Injustice."

For a few hours I forced myself to stay comparatively optimistic. But when a friend reported that the fire had reached our apartments, all of my optimism evaporated. I said a quick prayer as I ran outside, and then stood watching dumbfounded as flames raged over the area above our building. I wanted to react, but I had stifled my emotions for so long that when I finally needed them, I felt numb and empty.

Then I realized my lips were chapped. Rubbing them tenderly, I absentmindedly returned to the gym and asked around until I found somebody with Vaseline.™ Suddenly it hit me—during the few minutes I was concerned about my dry, chapped lips, I had forgotten about the crisis. In that moment, I realized God had allowed a trivial need to detach me from my apartment and my possessions. He took my mind away from the injustice I had perceived. And, although I had thought by doing my job I hadn't been allowed to take care of my own needs, God was taking care of them for me.

The rest of the night passed peacefully, and the morning brought with it testimony of our answered prayers—the fires had been contained just a few feet from our building and the campus was saved.

Lord,
thank You for the unexpected ways
in which You answer my prayers.
You alone know my needs
and You alone know how to care for them.
Thank You that You renew my strength in times of crisis.
Amen.

For you have not received a spirit of slavery leading to fear again,
but you have received a spirit of adoption
as sons by which we cry out,
"Abba, Father!"

Romans 8:15, NASB

Heavenly Daddy

Scott Sibley

One of my coworkers has a tri-lingual family. He and his wife immigrated from Eastern Europe and they often use their native tongue. They've lived in America for many years and speak English well, too. They're also Jews who have lived in Israel, so they speak Hebrew fluently. They can select the words and phrases from any of those three languages which will most accurately express their thoughts.

One summer, the son of this coworker was employed with us while he was home from college. We often got to witness the tension between their generations. The father had the traditions and values of the old country, while the son was a typical American college student. The father couldn't understand the son's ways; the son thought his father was out of touch with modern American ways. Their discussions were often lively and sprinkled with words and expressions foreign to the rest of us.

One day, they discussed their plans to go home from work, and then the son started to walk toward the door. Suddenly he turned to his father and said, "Abba, bring my radio."

At that moment I knew what the apostle Paul was trying to tell us when he said we can call God, "Abba." I'd heard that "Abba" means "Daddy," that it's the term Hebrew children call their fathers. But hearing a young man use it to get his father's attention really made the meaning of the verse clear.

God wants us to call him, "Abba." He wants us to know that we're His children. He wants to be our Daddy.

Often, I think so much of the majesty of God that I forget about His being my "Abba." When I come to Him in prayer, I think of Him as a king on the throne and I approach Him with great formality, sometimes even in fear. I think that He doesn't want to hear about my little concerns and problems.

"Abba, bring my radio." How I long for my relationship with God to be so close that I remember He is my Father, that I can sit with Him, and talk to Him about any little thought I have. I want to be so sure of His love that I think of Him as "Daddy."

Lord,
I want to draw close to You,
and love You as a child loves his own earthly father.
Remind me that You desire this, too,
and take away the barriers that keep me faraway from You.
Amen.

*Come now, you who say, "Today or tomorrow,
we shall go to such and such a city, and spend a year there and
engage in business and make a profit." Yet you do not know what
your life will be like tomorrow. You are just a vapor that appears
for a little while and then vanishes away.*

James 4:13–14, NASB

Tomorrow

Charles R. Swindoll

I was driving up to Forest Home with easy listening music crooning through the speaker, a quiet drive on a mellow Sunday afternoon. Then I saw something up ahead. Before I realized what it was, it flashed in my mind as something terribly wrong—out of place—distorted.

An overturned car—I could see it now. An ambulance screamed somewhere back. I felt as if someone had pushed a fist into my stomach. Directing traffic around the accident, a highway patrolman briskly motioned on the crawling line of cars. I got too close of a look at the vehicle resting on its crumpled top. The scene hangs in my mind: the bystanders staring in open-mouthed disbelief, two men dragging limp bodies out of the wreckage onto the pavement. All of the passengers were either dead or terribly mutilated.

Such a warm, peaceful Sunday. The day was bright and filled with leisure hours. But for three people, that moment the world flipped—violently, crazily, fatally—upside down. What appeared to be another day of "fun-'n'-games" became a day of infamous calamity. Naturally, I wondered if those victims knew our Lord and if they could smile at eternity.

Tomorrow. It may bring sickness, sorrow, or tragedy. It may announce an answer to your waiting prayer. It may introduce you to prosperity, the beginning of a friendship, a choice opportunity for sharing your Lord…or just another twenty-four hours of waiting, trusting, and claiming His presence. It may not even come. God may choose this very day to intervene and take you home—either by death or by rapture. We can speculate; we can dread; we can dream—but we do not know.

This sort of thinking leads to an inevitable question: Are you ready? "Ready for what?" you may ask. "Ready for anything" is my answer. Is your trust, your attitude of dependence, sufficiently stable to sustain you, regardless? Don't let the answer slip off your tongue too easily. Think about the implications of that question to your own life, health, job, and family.

Holy Father,
I pray that I will never forget the need to be ready to meet You.
Keep me prepared and directly focused
on the path of my eternal journey.
Amen.

I have learned to be content in whatever circumstances I am.
I know how to get along with humble means, and I also know how
to live in prosperity; in any and every circumstance I have learned
the secret of being filled and going hungry, both of having
abundance and suffering need.

Philippians 4:11–12, NASB

The Lord Sure Has Blest Us Good

Gene Wilder

The car and its passengers were a matched pair. The huge black sedan had outlived its glory. One could barely distinguish between the copper-colored rust and the streaks of red Georgia clay that adorned its dented fenders. The bumpers drooped unevenly like elderly limbs twisted by automotive arthritis.

The car's passengers weren't much better off. The tattered man could hardly lift the gas pump's nozzle to pump in his three-dollar purchase. I could tell he was poor and thought about offering to pay his bill, but something told me such a gesture might insult his pride. As I looked at the old gentleman, I felt sorry for him. I had so much. He had so little.

My sympathies were suddenly interrupted by the sound of an elderly woman's voice.

"Lawd, it sure is a perdy day, ain't it?" she said.

As I looked up, I was face to face with the old man's wife.

"Yes," she continued, "for eighty-two years the Lawd has blest me real good. And I ain't only old, but I'm in perdy good health, too! In fact, me and Henry is gittin' ready to go fishin'. Can you believe that? Eighty-two years old and still able to go fishin'. Yes, siree, the Lawd sure has blest us good!"

Before I could reply, Henry returned to the car and told his wife to quit her jabbering and come on. After a bump and grind, the engine, like its owners, found the momentum to start one more time.

As they pulled away, black smoke belched from under the tarnished bumpers, but I don't think the passengers noticed. They were too busy enjoying their divine blessings. They were too busy giving credit to *the Lawd who had blest them real good.* They were too busy goin' fishin' to notice their car, their poverty, or the feebleness that accompanied their accumulated years.

As their car disappeared in a cloud of black smoke, I refused to feel sorry for these two thankful saints. Those who have plenty and still want more are the ones to be pitied. For those who have much actually have very little unless they are thankful for what they possess. When one realizes that *the Lawd has blest them real good,* they need little more than a beat up old car, a worn pair of shoes, and a sunny day just made for fishin'.

Dear Lord,
please forgive me for thinking I'm not blessed unless I have more.
Help me to spend this day, and everyday,
being thankful to the Lord who has blest me real good.
In Jesus' name I pray.
Amen.

On the outside you appear good to everybody,
but inside you are full of hypocrisy and sins.

Matthew 23:28, TEV

Rusty Pipes

Harold J. Behm

The wall around the shower faucet showed dampness. It wasn't just a drippy faucet. There was probably a leak in the piping where it went through the wall. Another repair job for me was happening just two years after we moved in. I hadn't expected problems with the plumbing even though the house was ten years old. Our former house had galvanized iron water pipes that I knew would eventually rust through. This house had copper plumbing, so rusting pipes should not be a problem. No rusty pipes, no rusty water, at least that's what I thought when we purchased the house. The leak was small and not causing any major problem, so I procrastinated.

As a leak usually does, it gradually got worse. The time soon came when I had to act to save the whole wall from crumbling. I cut away the wall covering around the shower valve and also cut away the plaster board enough to locate the source of the moisture. Sure enough it was coming from the piece of pipe that went through the wall. Would copper pipe deteriorate like this? I tore into the wall further. Can you guess what I found? Instead of a brass connector, my all-copper plumbing had a short one-and-one-half-inch-long iron pipe connecting the copper plumbing to the brass shower valve. It was buried right in the plaster wall where no one would ever know—at least I'm guessing that's what the plumber thought when he installed it.

However, that little piece of iron pipe, buried in the wall and hidden from view, rusted completely through. I thought we had a rust-proof all-copper plumbing system, but there was a weak link, a hidden, weak link.

Our lives are frequently like this all-copper plumbing—everything in order, perfect behavior. But on the inside, ever so small, is an iron pipe that rusts. Little things can do great damage. We need to be aware that these weak links can exist. Because we're human, we should even expect them to appear. Then we will be ready to go to the proper source, the Word of God, for both repair and prevention.

Father,
I pray that if You see rust buried deep within me,
either physical or spiritual decay beginning its insidious action,
You will guide me through Your Word to whatever action
is required to remove this destructive influence.
Amen.

And Mary said,
"Behold, the bondslave of the Lord;
be it done to me according to your word."
And the angel departed from her.

Luke 1:38, NASB

The Dance of the Honeybee

Bruce M. Garner

The dance of the honeybee is something I've read about, but never expected to witness. The dance is the way researchers believe the honeybees communicate to other bees about food sources.

At the orchard I was visiting with a group of kindergarten and preschool students, a hive was built into a wall as part of a honey display. While perusing the assortment of honey offered for sale, you could also watch the bees at work. The kids were munching donuts and drinking cider, so I watched the bees.

A solitary bee flew into the hive and made her way to the mass of bees in the center. She began turning a series of figure eights while vibrating her tail. The other bees crowded around, but they didn't seem to be paying that much attention. If this bee had a message, it didn't look as if any of the others were receiving it. Then a remarkable thing happened. One bee broke away, crawled up to the exit, and flew out, heading for the nectar. A moment later, another did, and then another. Soon, six or seven bees left the hive, one by one.

The message of the honeybees tells us something about the message of the gospel. Though it may be preached to the masses, the response must be made by individuals, one by one. Though it often seems no one is listening, the message retains its power for those who receive it.

God still speaks to individuals and looks for our response to bring His life to others. Mary responded to the angel's message, and God used her to bear Christ. As we say yes to His message, we'll also be used to bear the life of Christ to our world.

Father,

help me to say yes to Your message,

and be a messenger of the Gospel.

Amen.

Thy word is a lamp to my feet
and a light to my path.

Psalm 119:105, NASB

All I Need

Robert Busha

For people who prefer hot water for their showers and having their beds in dry places, it may be difficult to comprehend the benefits of backpacking in the wilderness. My buddy, Chuck, and I have had many fireside discussions after long days on the trails of Isle Royale in the northern reaches of Michigan's Lake Superior. How others perceive our trips is one of many topics we've covered deep and wide. We remind ourselves that one of the many benefits comes from re-experiencing an absolute difference between wants and needs.

Imagine having sixty pounds of gear strapped to your back, including everything you need to survive for a couple of weeks—food, clothing, housing, bedding, cooking equipment, eating utensils, a water-filtering pump, and a few other items like a Bible, first-aid kit, camera, and industrial-strength mosquito repellent. Absent from our packs is a whole array of things from our homes and garages. And on the trail we don't contend with mortgages, car payments, taxes, or insurance premiums. Careers, family obligations, and social considerations are discussed, but they practically don't exist. Overall, the *shouldas* and *oughtas* that dominate our lives back home are fundamentally eliminated.

For a week or so, life becomes comparatively simple for us. Days are filled with taking just one step at a time on the trail as surely and safely as possible. Evenings are successful with the gathering of fire wood, eating a hot meal, relaxing weary bodies, and exploring the shoreline or fishing. At night sleep comes quickly.

With this simple list of supplies and our uncomplicated routine, all of our essential needs for living are met. Chuck and I have repeatedly found that at the beginning of our backpacking trips, within a short time on the trail, our minds and bodies make a conversion, giving preference to what is absolutely necessary to get by. The comforts and conveniences of home are put aside. What we needed or thought we needed a few hours before becomes excess baggage, mentally and physically.

It also seems there's a comparison on the trail with my spiritual needs. Denominations, churches, communities, and congregations often set standards and requirements that are actually greater than God requires of me.

What do I really need to carry with me spiritually each day in order to survive?

I must live by faith and abide by His Word. That's all! Keeping these two essential items with me will mean a much lighter and easier trip to my ultimate destination.

Father,

keep my eyes on Your Word,

and remind me that You are my guiding light

and comfort in all my endeavors.

Amen.

Meet Our Contributors

John Atherton and his family live in Rohnert Park, California. He and his wife, Pam, have one daughter, Holly, and two sons, Scott and Aaron. John's pastimes include music and gardening.

Harold Behm is a retired electrical engineer. He and his wife, Mary Jane, live in Charlotte, North Carolina. They have three grown daughters, each living in another state. His interests include writing, computers, photography, and woodworking.

Charles Blaker is retired from the faculty of Brookstone School in Columbus, Georgia. He is published on a wide range of topics in newspapers and magazines and is active in radio, television, theater drama, and modeling. Charles and his wife reside in Columbus.

Gary Bowker is director of development for Church Relations at Whitworth College in Spokane, Washington, where he lives with his wife, Carolyn. He has served as pastor in three states and was an Army chaplain in Vietnam, Korea, and Germany. He and Carolyn own an orchard, and Gary is the president of the Green Bluff Growers Association.

Robert Busha focuses on leadership for individual and organizational development, especially in the church. He and his wife, Mary Catherine, live and work in Santa Rosa, California. Their life seems to be almost totally consumed by helping bring books to life. Bob loves the mountains, the ocean, and hiking and backpacking in remote places.

John Calsin lives in West Chester, Pennsylvania. He is a freelance writer, newspaper columnist, essayist, and editorialist, "who works temporary jobs periodically to keep from starving." He is a member of the Greater Philadelphia Christian Writers' Fellowship and is a Sunday School teacher. He is recently married to Carol and loves it.

Tom Carter is the author of more than fifty articles and seven books, including *What Believers Must Know to Grow* and *For Members Only: A Guide to Responsible Church Membership*. He is the compiler and editor of *Spurgeon at His Best*. Tom is a pastor, living with his wife, Mary, their two daughters and one son in Dinuba, California.

Tim Coyle is pastor of Grace Brethren Church in Newark, Delaware, and an instructor at Truth Bible Institute. He is active with the Delaware Family Foundation. He and his wife, Mary, live in Bear, Delaware. He enjoys gardening (vegetables and roses) and has a special love for dogs, especially golden retrievers.

Jack Cunningham is a freelance writer based in Kenner, Louisiana. His work has appeared in *Young Salvationist, Christian Single, Vital Christianity, The Advocate, The Upper Room, Light from the Word,* and other publications. Jack's spare-time activities include golfing, fishing, and reading history.

James Dobson is founder and president of Focus on the Family. He and his wife, Shirley, parents of two grown children, live in Colorado Springs, Colorado. He is the author of *When God Doesn't Make Sense, The New Dare to Discipline, Straight Talk to Men and Their Wives, Love Must Be Tough,* and *Love for a Lifetime.*

Daniel Driver enjoys writing, public speaking, bowling, swimming, and reading—especially history and biographies. Dan is a directory assistance operator for U.S. West Communications. His home is in Mesa, Arizona.

Ronnie Floyd is the pastor of First Baptist Church of Springdale, Arkansas. He and his wife, Jena, have two sons, Joshua and Nicholas. He is the author of *Coping with Life in a Confused World*, and *Reconnecting: How to Renew and Preserve the Three Vital Elements of a Powerful Spiritual Life*.

Scott Froese is youth minister for the First Baptist Church in Neches, Texas. In addition, his small ranch keeps him busy. He enjoys watching and working with a few head of cattle that he and his dad own. Scott also teaches Sunday School.

Bruce Garner is associate pastor and administrator at Faith Tabernacle in Burton, Michigan. He and his wife, Sharon, have two daughters, Kelly and Haylee. He enjoys backpacking and camping with his family.

Dick Hagerman is a retired dentist. He and Dorothy, his wife of forty-six years, live in Wendell, Idaho. He has written for *Decision* magazine and *The Upper Room*, and for newspapers and magazines. He enjoys bow hunting and cross-stitching. Dick has also been a lay preacher and elder in the United Presbyterian Church.

James Harrison lives in Rancho Cordova, California. He is president of the Sacramento Christian Writers' Club, and he records taped books for the learning disabled and blind. Jim has taught in elementary school and served as pastor in United Methodist churches in Nevada and California.

David Hauk is an optometrist in group practice and lives in Reading, Pennsylvania, with his wife, Debra, and their three children. In addition to collecting foreign and ancient coins, and getting more serious about his writing, the majority of Dave's free time is taken up with his family...and he loves it.

Bill Hybels is pastor of Willow Creek Community Church in South Barrington, Illinois. He was also chaplain of the Chicago Bears for five years. He is the author of *Honest to God? Becoming an Authentic Christian, Too Busy Not to Pray,* and *Christians in a Sex-Crazed Culture*.

Larry Ladd lives in Hutchinson, Minnesota, with his wife and two children. He is an elementary school teacher and administrator and has been involved in Christian education and vocal music for many years.

Larry likes walking, gardening, and writing poetry. Larry and his wife are the owners of *Good News Unlimited Bible Book Center* in Hutchinson.

Max Lucado is heard weekly on the national radio program, "Up-Words." His many books include *God Came Near, And the Angels Were Silent, No Wonder They Call Him the Savior,* and *Six Hours One Friday.* He and his wife, Denalyn, live in San Antonio, Texas, with their three daughters. Max preaches at the Oak Hills Church of Christ.

Lt. Col. Louis Merryman (USAFR, Ret.) loves to watch movies and write plays, devotionals, and other articles, many of which have been published and performed. His latest play is *Ernie and the Christmas Angels.* He also likes hot air ballooning. Louis lives in El Segundo, California.

Dennis Meyers lives in Camarillo, California, with his wife, Barbara. He's an administrator with GTE California, a licensed private pilot, and loves "reading, bicycling, gardening, walking, and the Lord with all my heart."

Timothy Peter is a recent senior in journalism at John Brown University in Siloam Springs, Arkansas. Tim is a writer and editor for several university publications. He has been active in the Student Missionary Fellowship, Images (student drama ministry), and ROCK House Players (church youth drama ministry).

Gerry Presley is the worship leader and an elder with Grace Fellowship Church in Santa Rosa, California. In business, he is the used car sales manager for a large new car dealership in the city. Gerry and his wife, Aurora, have three children, Jennifer, Jason, and Jonathon.

Jason Presley is a senior English major at Pepperdine University in Malibu, California. His hobbies include making greeting cards; playing guitar, harmonica, and percussion instruments; and writing songs, poetry, fiction, and children's literature. He edits *Expressionists,* Pepperdine's literary and arts magazine.

Harold Sala is founder and president of Guidelines, Inc., an international Christian ministry reaching more than eighty countries through radio, television, seminars, and books. His spare-time pursuits include tennis, golf, and biking. He and his wife, Darlene, make their home in

Mission Viejo, California. Harold's recent books include *Today Can Be Different* and *Coffee Cup Counseling.*

Brad Sargent likes operatic whistling, puns, making people laugh, and hunting for out-of-print books. He lives in San Rafael, California, and is director of research for Exodus International, a world-wide network of Christian ministries. Brad serves on the board of directors of Christian AIDS Services Alliance.

Scott Sibley lives in King of Prussia, Pennsylvania, with his wife, Carol, and their three children. He is a professional engineer specializing in transportation projects including railroads, highways, and bus facilities. His hobbies are bicycling and home improvement projects. Scott is an elder in the First Presbyterian Church of Bridgeport, Pennsylvania.

Lester Smith is senior pastor of Richfield Road United Brethren in Christ Church in Flint, Michigan. He and his wife, Linda, have two children. Les has memorized and performs, in costume, twelve New Testament books. He has given presentations throughout America, in two foreign countries, and on Christian television.

Robert Smith is pastor of Calvary Baptist Church in Compton, California. He has written numerous magazine articles and has recently contracted with the National Baptist Convention to publish his book, *The Hebrew Names for God,* and with Baker Books for his book *Blacks and Cults.* He and his wife, Margaret, live in Pasadena. Robert loves church league basketball, reading, and writing.

Chuck Swindoll is pastor of First Evangelical Free Church in Fullerton, California, and president of the Dallas Theological Seminary in Texas. Chuck and his wife, Cynthia, have four adult children. He has written more than twenty best-selling books including *The Quest for Character, Flying Closer to the Flame: A Passion for the Holy Spirit,* and *Come Before Winter and Share My Hope.*

Richie Thomas and his wife, Reba, live in Burton, Michigan, where he is the senior pastor at Faith Tabernacle, a metropolitan church enjoying rapid growth. Richie likes music, writing, and amateur sports, and is a fan of hot weather and wide fairways.

Russ Wagner lives in Westland, Michigan, with his wife, Laura, and their two sons, Daniel and Nathan. He is a warehouse manager for an industrial medical supply company. Russ loves outdoor activities, especially hiking and bicycling.

Mark Weinrich is a Christian and Missionary Alliance pastor in Truth or Consequences, New Mexico. Over 280 of his poems, short stories, and articles have been accepted for publication. Four of his early reader books and three juvenile mysteries are soon to be released. When he's not writing, Mark likes hiking, collecting Indian artifacts, exploring caves, and backpacking.

Peter West and his wife, Vera, live in Golden Valley, Minnesota. He is pastor emeritus of First Baptist Church in Minneapolis. Peter enjoys photography and fishing and serving as a board member on the Greater Minneapolis Association of Evangelicals. He is the author of the book *Men of Faith* and has written articles appearing in *Decision* magazine.

Gene Wilder is pastor of the First Baptist Church in Fitzgerald, Georgia. He and his wife, Patricia, and their two teenage children live in nearby Lizella. In addition to his writing, Gene likes reading, skiing, golfing, and singing, as well as music composition and performance.

Dave Wilkerson is the pastor of Times Square Church in New York City and the president of World Challenge, Inc. He and his wife, Gwen, have two sons who are both ministers. Their two daughters are ministers' wives. Dave is the author of *The Cross and the Switchblade*.

Grayson Wyly, father of four and grandfather of seven children, retired from the 3M Company in 1989, after twenty-five years. He worked in researching insulating tapes. In addition to writing, he also enjoyed swimming, boating, fishing and gardening. Grayson died October 22, 1992. His widow, Louise, resides in Minneapolis.

Credits

The following articles are used by permission of the publishers.

"Spiritual Frustrations" by James Dobson was adapted from *When God Doesn't Make Sense* by James Dobson, © 1993 James Dobson, Inc. Used by permission of Tyndale House Publishers, Inc. All rights reserved.

"You Can't Outgive the Lord" by James Dobson was adapted from the book *Love for a Lifetime* by James Dobson, © 1987 by James C. Dobson. Published by Multnomah Press, Portland, OR 97266. Used by permission.

"The Disposition We Share" by Ronnie W. Floyd was adapted from the book *Reconnecting* by Ronnie W. Floyd. (Nashville: Broadman & Holman Publishers, 1993), 8–11. All rights reserved. Used by permission.

"Discipline" by Bill Hybels was adapted from the book *Honest to God?* by Bill Hybels. © 1990 by Bill Hybels. Used by permission of Zondervan Publishing House.

"Eternal Instants" by Max Lucado was adapted from the book *God Came Near* by Max Lucado, © 1987 by Max Lucado. Used by permission of Multnomah Books, Questar Publishers.

"A Downward Spiral" by Charles R. Swindoll was adapted from the book *The Quest for Character* by Charles R. Swindoll. © 1982 by Charles R. Swindoll, Inc. Used by permission of Zondervan Publishing House.

"Tomorrow" by Charles R. Swindoll was adapted from the book *Second Wind* by Chuck Swindoll. © 1977 by Charles R. Swindoll, Inc. Used by permission of Zondervan Publishing House.

"Crisis Training" by David Wilkerson was adapted from the newsletter *Times Square Church Pulpit Series* by David Wilkerson, "Getting Back Your Fight" (October 25, 1993). Used by permission.